THE BIG BOOK OF
DUMMIES, REBELS
AND OTHER GENIUSES

Jean-Bernard Pouy & Serge Bloch

Anne Blanchard

THE BIG BOOK OF DUMMIES, REBELS AND OTHER GENIUSES

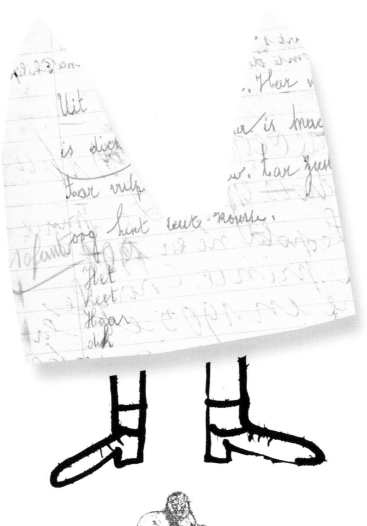

ENCHANTED LION BOOKS

First American Edition published in 2008 by
Enchanted Lion Books, 201 Richards Street, Studio 4, Brooklyn, NY 11231

Originally published in French as *L'Encyclopédie des Cancres, rebelles et autres génies* by Jean-Bernard Pouy, Serge Bloch and Anne Blanchard, © Éditions Gallimard Jeunesse, 2006

Translation © 2008 Enchanted Lion Books
Translated by Claudia Bedrick

[A CIP record is on file with the Library of Congress]

ISBN-10: 1-59270-103-5
ISBN-13: 978-1-59270-103-2

Printed in China

To all of those
who have sat dreaming
in front of the radiator

CONTENTS

Ss, Ss, Ss, Ss, Ss, Ss, Ss, Ss, Ss, Ss,

Ss, Ss, Ss, Ss, Ss, Ss, Ss, Ss, Ss, Ss,

Preface 8

Armstrong 10

Balzac 14

Bell 18

Buffon 22

Cézanne 26

Chaplin 30

Charlemagne 34

Christie 38

Churchill 42

Da Vinci 46

Dali 52

Darwin 56

David-Néel 60

Débussy 64

Disney 68

Ll, Ll, Ll, Ll, Ll, Ll, Ll, Ll, Ll,

Ll, Ll, Ll, Ll, Ll, Ll, Ll, Ll, Ll,

Dumas 72

Dunant 76

Edison 80

Einstein 84

Flaubert 88

Gouges 92

Lennon 96

Lincoln 100

London 104

Picasso 108

Truffaut 112

Bibliography 116

Picture Credits 122

Authors 124

Acknowledgements 125

PREFACE

Who would have bet on them when they were young?

Here is a portrait gallery of men and women who left their mark on literature, the arts, the sciences, and history, despite their chaotic beginnings.

At school, many were declared mediocre, incompetent, slow—in a word, dummies! Others barely went to school. At home, and later at work, they were despaired of. But while their rebellious character exasperated all who knew them, they dreamed near a warm radiator or took multiple detours before finding their own path.

Over time, history has bestowed genius and fame upon them. Many have come to dominate our culture, looming over us with their great, almost sacred presence. Encyclopedias describe them in hushed and serious tones, their pockets stuffed with virtues. But these pockets are more unevenly stitched than might be guessed.

So let us rediscover twenty-six of the great names here from a new perspective, through reading about their impudent youth. Their early years were marked by incidents funny and moving by turn. Their autobiographies, letters, and other writings, which we have plundered for you, bear witness to this. Seen in this way, these icons become human and flawed once again, allowing us to look on with amusement and tenderness. The drawings of Serge Bloch portray them in a similar fashion.

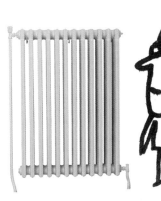

In addition, short sidebars present basic facts and further details. These entries tell how and why these names left their mark: inventions; revolutionary equations; good deeds; great novels; musical innovations; celebrated paintings; or cult films.

What cannot be found here are typical or perfect paths. Instead, chance and luck often played a role, with these individuals born at a time or in a place that allowed them to develop their talents, or at least didn't hinder them. And then there is the mystery of personality, revealed by the passion, appetite, will, and determination that carried them along their seemingly unreasonable and highly uncertain paths.

One might fairly ask, did any of these figures really have a choice about submitting to their passion, exerting their exacting intelligence, or devoting their life to what eventually revealed itself as a seemingly inborn gift? These individuals serve neither as examples nor models.

Rather, *The Big Book of Dummies, Rebels and Other Geniuses* raises an eyebrow at its subjects, refreshing and enlivening their great names, while inviting us to smile at the unruliness of childhood and the modest zigzags of each of us!

For in the end, what would a life without detours or wasted time really be like ?

LOUIS ARMSTRONG

As a child, I was called both "Dipper" and "Satchmo" (from "Dippermouth" and "Satchelmouth"), but it was "Satchmo" that stuck. These names were perhaps one way of suggesting that later on I would play the trumpet. I was born in New Orleans on August 4, 1901, in James Alley, in the croweded Back O'Town section that was for Blacks only. (A story in itself.) At the time, this neighborhood was called *"the battlefield."* My mother *"told me that the night I was born there was a great big shooting scrape in the Alley and the two guys killed each other."*

We lived in a poor, rundown shack, buffeted by windy drafts in the winter and stiflingly hot in the summer. As for my dad, he had already taken off. Mayann, my mother, wasn't even twenty. To feed her two little ones (my baby sister and me), she most likely took advantage of one of the principal occupations available in what was *"a hot quarter."* In my neighborhood, everybody lived together, *"...churchpeople, gamblers, hustlers, cheap pimps, thieves, prostitutes and lots of children."*

As a young kid, I just hung around. To keep me from taking a bad, even criminal turn, I was entrusted to my grandmother, Josephine, who took good care of me and tried to give me a little education while doing the laundry of the white folks for whom she worked. Toward that end, she sent me to Church and Sunday school, where I did a lot of singing. I loved to sing and by the age of seven, I already belonged to a little group called "The Singing Fools." My pals and I collected pennies and nickels by belting out songs on street corners. In the streets where I spent most of my time, my ears were filled with the endless music that floated on the air, and I was filled with admiration for the

LOUIS ARMSTRONG (1901-1971),
American. A trumpet player of genius with
a voice like no other, he is held to be the
inventor of vocal jazz, as well as one of the
most influential artists in jazz history.

lively brass bands that crisscrossed the neighborhood. It was a party that never ended, with all of the different sounds and melodies blending together. New Orleans was a place that relieved its misery through music.

From age nine until twelve, I spent nearly all of my time playing music on the streets and doing odd jobs. That ended on December 31, 1913. It was New Year's eve and I was out in the beautiful evening, kidding around with a .38 revolver that I had lifted from my stepfather. To make my buddies laugh, I shot it off right in the middle of the street. Boom! With that, I found myself before a judge who sent me to a reform school called the Colored Waif's Home for Boys. There I had a stroke of good fortune, as one of the supervisors, Peter Davis, was also a music instructor. He was hard on me at first, but he eventually allowed me to participate in the chorus, and then in the Home's brass band as the cornet player. He also made it my job to blow the bugle every morning to wake everyone up! I was at the Home long enough to be promoted to bandleader. I was released from the reformatory after a stay of 18 months and, believe it or not, I was sad to go.

Once out, I returned to my neighborhood. As I was fourteen, there was nothing else for me to do but get a job. I worked as a coal deliverer and junkman, but I held myself together by playing the blues at night in the local dives and honky tonks, where I made real progress. Boy did I have breath! Finally I met a real, big-time jazzman named Joe "King" Oliver, who quickly had it with hearing me blow into second rate instruments. Taking me under his wing, this god offered me my first real cornet!

In 1917, with the U.S. at war, my neighborhood

(Storyville)—too poor, too dangerous, and too Black—was closed down as a threat. All of the musicians had to leave, along with everyone else. This was hard, since for many it involved leaving the warm country of the South for the factories of the North. I stayed in New Orleans for a while, before going on foot from club to club, ending up in St. Louis and also on the riverboats of the Mississippi. In 1922, Papa Joe, who played regularly in the dance halls and speakeasies of Chicago, sent for me. What a shock! *"All those big buildings: I thought they were universities."* Nevertheless, I fit in quickly. I played more strongly than ever, with more inventiveness and more freedom. Before long, I had triumphed! Soon after that, my band started to make records, and I—a dream come true—played with all of the "greats": Sidney Bechet, Jelly Roll Morton, Earl Hines and many others. While my band and I continued to make music, suddenly, without warning or even my wanting it, our style was labeled "New Orleans" jazz, a name that stuck.

The rest is history. From then on, my life was all music and the joy of giving a good show. The "Satchelmouth," raised in extreme poverty with no formal education to speak of, would become a mouth and a voice of gold, known throughout the entire world.

How jazz was born.
The European settlers who peopled North America quickly realized that sugarcane, cotton and tobacco grew well in the heat and fertile soil of the South as well as in The Antilles. But the manual labor for cultivating these crops was lacking. The enormous traffic in Africans——the slave trade—was developed in response to this need. Millions of Africans were bought and sold and brought to North America, which was vastly enriched by their free labor. The slaves, converts to Christianity, took to gospel singing to express themselves. Infusing these songs with the traditional rhythms of their African cultures, they evoked their "blues"——their sorrows and their sufferings. It was from this encounter between traditional African music and European hymns that jazz was born.

HONORÉ DE BALZAC

The colossal *Human Comedy*.
Balzac already had had success when the first title in his *Human Comedy* came out in 1842. Between 1789 and 1848, French society passed through the crucible. Paris, the provinces, all social classes and generations, as well as nearly all professions are evoked in Balzac's *Comedy*. Also on display is the great ambition of the author, the tireless, nocturnal toiler, who consumed vast quantities of coffee to work through the night. The novelist didn't spare anything in creating the characters that seem so strikingly real to readers. For Balzac, they also, of course, took on life. As the story goes, when Balzac was dying, he was so fully taken over by the illusion that he had created that he called out for the help of none other than Dr. Horace Bianchon, the great doctor from *The Human Comedy*.

No, no, it is I who am honored. Really. Please sit down. I have so many things to tell you, enough for a novel really, but a real one. A memoir, perhaps, but one similar to my fiction. I was born in 1799 in Tours, France. My father was in the military administration and my mother belonged to the provincial bourgeoisie. After me, they had two more children—two daughters, Laure and Laurence. My mother also gave me a brother, Henry, but she conceived him with her lover. That's how it was in the provinces. You have only to read my books, where relationships are even more complicated.

My sister, Laure, and I were sent to a wet nurse in the countryside. We were too tiring for mama. In any case, she greatly preferred socializing with her lady friends in town. As for my father, he was only interested in his work. Therefore, when my sister and I returned to the family home, we were hidden away on the third floor under the watchful eye of a ferocious dragon, our governess Madame Delahaye. At this safe distance, we didn't bother anyone during parties or receptions. I was four at the time and Laure was three. Our only sweet moments were when we went to Paris to visit our mother's parents. Our grandparents were gentle and kind, and they had an adorable dog named Mouche.

When it was time for me to start school, I went to a boarding school as a day student. By the time I was eight, however, I found myself boarding at a school far away in Vendôme. My life there, learning about Charlemagne and other historical figures and discipline from as far back as Attila, was not a pleasure. Moreover, I never left school, not even for vacations. Additionally, I had to wear a uni-

HONORÉ DE BALZAC (1799-1850),
French writer, who depicted the society and
people of his time in his magnificent Human
Comedy. This huge series of ninety-five
novels consists of no fewer than 2,000
characters. These return from one novel to
the next, which was a new idea at the time.

form like in the army, and I was allowed to write to my parents only once a month. Furthermore, there were no visits: *"They soften the character."* Over six years, I saw my parents only twice, which was probably just as well. To understand this, you have only to read my novel *Louis Lambert*, which gives a full account. And then there were the punishments: blows to the knees and harsh raps to the fingers. As for rewards, I was unfamiliar with those, since I was considered a clumsy, chubby, timid, parasitic, and melancholy child. I was punished because I detested my school, which I found to be unjust. The other children agitated me and collective life stifled me. I honestly wished that my parents would forget me entirely and stop sending me pocket money, since my work was poor and I was stubborn. *"Nothing attracts him, neither lessons nor homework. Unconquerable repugnance in the face of mandatory work."* That was how the headmaster summed things up. Fortunately, in the somber gathering of stormy clouds, there is always a little corner of blue that peaks through. In my case, the blue sky was a priest, Hyacinthe-Laurent Lefebvre, who attempted to catch my interest with mathematics, but with whom I set about reading books from his library in secret. This became my passion!

Henceforth, all I did was read. All at once, I ceased to do anything else, and I was punished more and more often. I was even put into a sort of minuscule dungeon called, "the wooden rump." This didn't bother me, however, because in there I was able to read peacefully and continue on my quest. As I had a prodigious memory, I retained everything, and this allowed me to begin to write. At first I tried to do the same thing as my beloved authors. My first manuscript, which I believe was called *Treatise on the*

Père Goriot left to his sad thoughts

The laws that govern people and society. Before beginning to write, the novelist has to study his subject for a long time, and as he does so, his observations feed into his notes, which multiply in his desk drawer. Next the author synthesizes and creates. In his novels, Balzac interpreted reality, seeking to explain the workings of the world. Like a scientist, he believed that he had discovered its laws: the desire for money and power leads the dance in every society, which, in essence, is simply *"a union of fools and rogues."* He also fathomed how deeply people are governed by fixed ideas (to be a good father: *Père Goriot*; to become an artist: *Lost Illusions*). For the most part, Balzac's characters are driven to ruin, madness or death by their illusions.

Will, was confiscated. The punishments were endless. I no longer even talked to my schoolmates. I rejected everything that I was taught. On the other hand, everything that I learned on my own impassioned me. Over what seemed an eternity (and eternity feels very, very long), I was shadowed by my reputation as a poor student.

Little by little, I sank into a kind of madness and was kicked out of school. I was fourteen years old. I was ecstatic about returning home to my sister, Laure, who was the only one who noticed me. *"Honoré resembled one of those sleepwalkers who sleeps with his eyes open.... Without the knowledge of his professors, he had read through most of the school's library...."* Once home, I repeated the offence. Straightaway, I attacked the shelves of my father's study, digging in deep where they were most disordered and full of philosophers: Rousseau, Voltaire, even Chateaubriand, that big idiot. By this time it was clear that I had a fixed idea. I wanted to write.

Although I wasted time at school and again at the Faculty of Law where I later went, I still managed to write a tragedy about Cromwell by the time I was twenty. My father gave it to a scholar to read. His verdict was without appeal: the author should do whatever possible other than write. That fool! He couldn't even see the essential, that what I wanted to do was to write! It's true that one can't simply say that. All the same, it's easy to understand, isn't it?

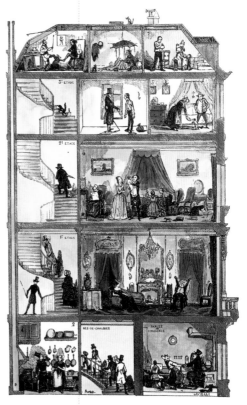

Useless details and descriptions?
Balzac's novels fall from the hands of those who find his descriptions interminable and burdened with details. From the opening pages on, the reader cannot overlook anything about the main character: physical characteristics, habits, tastes, profession and domestic life all are scrutinized. Indeed, in the novelist's view, the very character and way of life of each of his protagonists can be translated into what we see of them. Let's take a character's physique, for example: the thin have a good chance of being unhappy or swallowed up and the fat of being happy. Balzac, however, was not only a powerful observer, but also a remarkable storyteller. Thus a restless reader can always skim the descriptive passages in order to jump into the plot.

ALEXANDER GRAHAM BELL

What will the fellow who has a grandfather who's a recognized elocutionist, a father who's a professor of diction, a mother who's hard-of-hearing and becomes deaf, and a wife who's a deaf-mute end up doing? Ding-a-ling-a-ling. He will invent the telephone, of course.

This fellow's name is Alexander Graham Bell, and he was born in 1847 in Edinburgh, Scotland. His father, Melville, was a wonderful storyteller, but his mother was unable to hear his stories. In her own right, however, she was a painter and an accomplished pianist. The Bells were a tight family that made music together, took photographs (already!) and put on pantomimes.

As a boy, he was called Aleck. Educated at home, he didn't have to go to school until the age of ten. Although Aleck enjoyed reading and writing from a young age, what he enjoyed most was wandering around and exploring. One day as he was doing just that "*...he heard the murmur of the wheat as it undulated. Having gone into a wide field, he found himself lost. Panicked, he went here and there in every direction. Night began to fall. Where were his parents? ...In tears, he lay down, his ear to the ground. The silence gave way to the sound of wind. He sobbed and went limp, when—miracle!—he heard a sound from far away: 'Aleck! Aleck!' It was the muffled voice of his father that the earth carried to him.*"

Okay, we're still far from texting...oh right, from the telephone. True enough, but let's continue.

At age fifteen, Aleck finished school (he went for about five years) with an unremarkable record that greatly disappointed his demanding father. The only subject in which Aleck had any interest was science. Fleeing his father, he left for London to join his grandfather, a former

The telephone is born.
In 1876, while working on an artificial ear for the deaf, Bell succeeded in transmitting the human voice the length of an electrical cable by code. This was the result of many years of research into the function of sound and electricity. His great discovery was that by modulating the intensity of electrical current—instead of opening and closing the connection as is done with a telegraphic line—it would be possible to faithfully transmit sound, including that of the human voice! Bell's telephone microphone, like a human eardrum, possessed a membrane that vibrated at the sound of the voice.

ALEXANDER GRAHAM BELL (1847-1922),
a Scottish-born inventor, has come down in history as the inventor of the telephone.
The invention of the telephone launched a new era of technological communication
that continues to shape our world today. Bell was also a teacher who worked with
the deaf in innovative and noteworthy ways.

cobbler, theater actor, orator, elocutionist, and teacher. Mercifully, his grandfather let him do whatever he wanted. Together they read aloud from Shakespeare for hours on end. Aleck's happiness was total. This lasted for one year.

On his return to Scotland, Aleck didn't get along any better with his father. Nevertheless, his dad took him to see a demonstration of a speaking machine, following which he challenged Aleck and his older brother, Melville, to build a similar sort of talking automaton. Simple! The two lads set to work, trying to figure out how the organs of speech (tongue, mouth, throat) function. "*For want of details about the vocal chords, they sacrificed the family cat, following which they went to the butcher's for a sheep's larynx in order to study it's anatomy.*" Using all sorts of things—wood, cotton, thin sheets of rubber, a bellows and a funnel—they created a lifelike head that did, in fact, speak. Using the bellows to force air through the windpipe, they made the automaton utter the word, "mama." The sound was so real that the neighbors thought there was a baby in the house! Aleck also experimented with the family dog, Trouve, manipulating its mouth and vocal chords so that its continuous growl (which Aleck taught it to make) was heard as words.

Following this, Aleck arranged to leave again. He made it as far as the north of Scotland, to Elgin, where he became a student-teacher in a school for boys. While taking classes himself, he taught both music (he was a super pianist like his mom) and diction. He was eighteen—only slightly older than his students. Next, he taught at the old University of Bath, after which he went to London, where he studied at the University and taught deaf children. He also continued with his curious passions, going so far as

"Hamlet calling": Bell's telephone makes its debut.

For Bell, the consecration of his invention came on June 25, 1876, at the time of an exhibition in Philadelphia when the emperor of Brazil tried his telephone. The inventor called the emperor from about one hundred yards away. The emperor was doubtful: was it really Bell on the other end of the line delivering a monologue from *Hamlet*? Finally convinced, the emperor exclaimed to the company at large: "*It speaks! It speaks!*" As early as 1877, the Bell Telephone Company was created to loan telephones and operate a small network.

to assist in surgical operations in order to understand the anatomical mysteries of speech. Equally enthusiastic about electricity, he installed a telegraph between his house and that of a friend. He also perfected one of his father's own inventions, which involved the pronunciation of 34 basic sounds and was intended to help four deaf girls learn how to pronounce brief phrases.

However, in 1870, tragedy befell the Bells when Aleck and his brothers fell gravely ill with tuberculosis. Aleck's two brothers died in a period of four months. Shortly before their deaths, "*in a moment of fever, the brothers promised each other that whoever should die first would try to communicate from the beyond.*" Following this terrible loss, the Bells left for Canada, taking Aleck to purer air. On the boat, Aleck became fascinated by a book called *On the Sensations of Tone*, by the German physicist von Helmholtz. Barely able to read German, Aleck understood the book to suggest that vowel sounds, and hence speech, could be transmitted electrically. This misunderstanding was a lucky mistake, for it inspired him with the idea for his telephone!

Taking off from there, spurred on by his study of the human voice, his interest in electrical waves, and his love for Mabel, a young deaf woman soon to be his wife, Aleck perfected his telephone early in 1876. On February 14, he submitted his patent application. Somewhat later his rival Alisha Gray (a name in telegraphy) declared, "*Bell's speaking telephone is a nice toy for science types, but it has no commercial interest and provides nothing more than the telegraph.*"
Oh really? It's tough when someone beats you to the punch.

Inventors and inventions: when newness is in the air.
Having succeeded in his first communication, Bell decided to apply for a patent. His main rival, Alisha Gray, applied for a patent on a similar invention just hours later. While Bell is popularly known as the inventor of the telephone, the U.S. Congress made a statement in 2002 recognizing retrospectively that this title really belongs to Antonio Meucci, who tested his telephone system sixteen years before Bell's was finished. Despite this statement, the issue continues to inspire heated debate.

BUFFON

"**A** man should be considered as nothing for the first fifteen years of his life," wrote Buffon as an old man. As far as his early life goes, it's true that we don't know much about it.

Georges-Louis Leclerc (GL for short) was born in Bourgogne in 1707, the first of five children. His mother, Anne-Christine Marlin, an intelligent and vivacious woman, educated him at home to begin with. GL was so inspired by her that later in life he wrote some real nonsense: "*Intelligence is most often transmitted from mother to son....*" His father, Benjamin-François, was a magistrate with a talent for business. When GL was ten, his mother inherited a large sum of money and property, of which Buffon was one of the estates. This allowed her husband to become lord of Buffon as well as a counselor in the Burgundian parliament. The family moved to Dijon and all was well. As for GL, he went to a Jesuit College in Godrans, where he was considered, "*studious but hardly brilliant.*" He was poor in French, a little better in Latin and ancient Greek, and, with good instruction, he did well in science. His classmates found him clumsy, more gifted at physics than physical education.

It quickly became clear that mathematics was all that mattered to the young GL. He even claimed to have discovered the binomial theorem (Newton) on his own. He read all of Euclid, along with the *Analysis of the Infinitely Small* by the Marquis de l'Hospital, and he became a fan of infinitesimal calculus. His first misfortune was that no one was interested in this little question. His second misfortune was that his father was determined to see him follow in his footsteps. Thus, with sorrow in his heart, the young GL enrolled at the Faculty of Law in Dijon. Luckily, he made two buddies who were as impatient with

A thousand rungs of research.
The 36 volumes of Buffon's *Natural History*, which appeared between 1749 and 1788, elaborated a theory of evolution for the living world. Some of his colleagues reproached him for his audacity, since as a scientist he had developed hypotheses in scientific areas in which he had little expertise. Many philosophers argued about the implications of his work. As for the authorities and the theologians, they were shocked that he called into question the literal reading of Creation as set forth in the Bible. Others, however, took his part, leading Buffon's opponents and partisans to publicly confront each other.

GEORGES-LOUIS LECLERC
DE BUFFON (1707-1788),
*French scientist and the director of the Jardin des
Plantes in Paris, aroused the curiosity of generations
of readers and prepared the way for a number of
investigations with his immense Natural History,
General and Particular. His ambition: to describe
and explain the history of the earth and of life in its
totality. His view influenced two generations of natu-
ralists, including Lamarck and Darwin.*

the dryness of legal texts as he. Instead of focusing
on law, the three friends frequented the circle of a
local intellectual who had an astounding library
(35,000 volumes) and was friendly with the local philosophers. All the same, GL succeeded in obtaining his law
degree in 1726 at the age of nineteen. Not bad!

His law degree changed nothing, however, as it was math
alone that counted. He corresponded with the Swiss

mathematician, Gabriel Cramer (a big shot), who helped him to gain recognition in an extremely closed milieu. This allowed GL to fantasize about abandoning the magistracy before he even had begun. His parents were opposed to this, however, and probably shouted, *"There aren't any openings in the sciences!"* Nevertheless, the young GL persisted, and his parents' antics made him want to leave home all the more. *"One needs only to leave home to become worthwhile...and to be respected and liked at the level of one's merit...I will do all I can to keep away from Dijon for as long as possible."* In the end his parents relented, allowing him to enroll in the Faculty of Medicine in Angers. Upon reflection, they had decided that of all the sciences, medicine was the most serious.

At the Medical Faculty, GL continued with mathematics, while discovering botany and zoology. He even took up hiking (whoa!) to familiarize himself with plants and herbs. Likewise he took to studying the female up close, to the point that he fought a duel, killed his rival, and had to escape from Angers. With that, his medical studies came to an end. His return to Dijon was something of a cold shower. Fortunately, the intellectual circle to which he had belonged was still active and his friends were still there. In any case, it was an exciting time thanks to his newly acquired passion for natural history. Also, with school behind him, he finally was able to travel. In 1730, along with a British friend and his tutor, GL set out to tour France, Italy and England. His year of pleasure and discovery (he loved the nature he saw, but the ruins of Rome left him cold) ended when he learned of his mother's death and returned to Dijon. However, he left quickly again right after, this time for Geneva in order to meet Cramer in person.

A solid citizen.

Buffon divided his time between Paris and Bourgogne. A rich man, he had a chateau built on the Buffon property and, with time, was made a noble. In his park, he put a menagerie, laboratory, and ironworks, which allowed him to concentrate on scientific matters. He also created a nursery to carry out research, which won him the favor of the king. This was because the king's minister to the Navy needed scientists with whom to consult about improving the construction of war ships. The first scientists consulted did not have means of carrying out precise experiments, but Buffon did. To assist the Navy, Buffon studied the tensile strength (the resistance of a material to extreme force) of timber. His assistance to the king significantly helped his nomination to the Academy of Sciences in 1739.

Still strong in math, GL knew how to add things up when faced with his mother's death. By opposing his father's remarriage, he was able to recuperate his inheritance, which included the lands of Bourgogne. With this, GL became Buffon, a man of property and distinction. One day as he was searching for mushrooms on his newly won lands, he had an epiphany, realizing that his true task was to devote himself to the natural sciences.

Henceforth, Buffon worked like a madman, dividing his time between Bourgogne and Paris, where he discussed the latest discoveries in science and philosophy (most notably with Voltaire) and tried to advance his career. Given the post of overseeing the King's Gardens in Paris (now the Jardin des Plantes), he developed those collections into the Museum of Natural History, an extraordinary feat. And despite his problems with the Church, with which he disagreed about God's role in creating the world (everywhere he looked he saw natural causes), he nevertheless was made a count by Louis XV.

One of his naturalist colleagues had this to say about him: "...*his imagination carries him away but he knows not how to analyze.*" Envy or insight? It's hard to say. All the same, his monumental work of *Natural History, General and Particular* is significant, concerning as it does—everything, absolutely everything (the solar system, minerals, plants, animals, humans, etc.). Marvelously written, it's a mish-mash of illuminations ("*among humans there are no races, just one species tinted the color of the climate*"), borrowings from colleagues, and understandable errors.

He certainly was no buffoon, Buffon!

Great Hall of Evolution at the Natural History Museum in Paris

Organizing the living world.
Buffon looked closely at the environment, history and habits of the species that he studied. He grouped together many species that were physiologically close, but had different behaviors or habits. He constituted families based on biological unity. From this he concluded that families with the same biological unity are all the issue of the same unique species that transformed over time. Otherwise put, the tiger and cat are the descendents of the same family of felines. This idea can be found again and again up until Darwin. What Darwin shared with Buffon was his belief that everything develops through natural phenomena and that life on earth came about in this way as well.

PAUL CÉZANNE

To Paris!
For the artists of the 19th century (even of the early 20th), the act of leaving home was something like a second birth. To leave family and the world of childhood behind was to say goodbye to a provincial way of life where one had to conform and behave according to very clear rules of right and wrong. In Paris, where the wealthy spent their money on shows, books and paintings, everything seemed possible. Throughout the 19th century and into the early 20th, Paris was the capital of art and of the quarrels about what art should be. Every year, during the major exhibition called the "Salon," painters showed their canvases, hoping for success with the public. Cézanne was refused access to the Salon for many years. When he became famous in his fifties, he had already been back in Provence for a long time.

Born in Aix-en-Provence in January 1839, Paul was both a southerner and a Capricorn, the sign of those who realize themselves late. Perhaps you don't go in for astrology? Well, that's all right, since Paul can still be called a late bloomer.

Paul's father was a small-town banker, which is important, since papa wanted his son to follow in his footsteps. *"Cézanne the banker cannot see without trembling/Born behind the bank a painter to come,"* noted the young Cézanne. Paul wrote a lot, and, for better or worse, he almost always wrote in verse.

Paul received a good classical education (along the lines of Latin and Greek) and did well, so to begin with he did not disappoint his gruff and authoritarian father. He also managed to have a good time as a young student, particularly with his friend Emile Zola, who, of course, became just as famous as he.

Paul met Emile in the courtyard of their high school when he defended him against the teasing of some classmates. The small, skinny Zola brought Paul some apples the next day, and they quickly became fast friends. (The apples also are worth noting given how many of them Paul painted over the course of his career.)

With a third friend, Baptistin, who later became an astronomer, they formed an inseparable trio, whiling away their time together by wandering through the beautiful countryside, swimming in the rivers, reading poetry aloud and daydreaming. They also formed a band, *Les Gais Lurons* (something like, The Happy-Go-Luckies) in which Paul played the cornet and Emile the clarinet.

A happy childhood, or almost, clouded only by the dreaded baccalauréate exams (required to go from high school

PAUL CÉZANNE (1839-1906), French painter, who rendered humans, nature and objects in a completely new way by representing them geometrically. Through his radical approach to painting, Cézanne paved the way for Cubist painters such as Picasso. After Cézanne, painting was no longer what it had been.

A moderm Olympia

When the novelist Zola described the bohemian world, Cézanne saw red! The young people who went to Paris to try their hand at literature, music, and painting lived poorly, but happily. Coined from "bohemian," the expression "bohemianism" was created to designate this artistic underworld. It is this world that Zola described in his novel, Work. Of all the bohemian characters that Zola created for his book, the painter is the darkest. Tenacious and relentless in revolutionizing his art, as well as more solitary than the others, Zola's painter ends by hanging himself in front of one of his canvases. When he read Work, Cézanne, who had known difficult periods in his youth, recognized himself in the painter. It was for this reason that he broke definitively with Zola, his childhood friend.

to college) that Paul faced in 1858. Paul wrote a poem about his dread. Though not a part of his standard biography, it speaks eloquently to his state of mind at the time: "I tremble when I see all of Geography,/History, Latin, Greek, and Geometry/conspire against me:/I see them menacing/The examiners whose piercing looks/Carry profound turmoil and confusion straight into my heart/ My fear at each instant terribly intensified." Not quite a masterpiece? Exactly...

All the same, a miracle occurred, and Paul passed his exams, not at first, but when he took them for a second time.

"Yes, my dear, yes, my dear, a very great joy,
With this new title in my heart deployed,
Of Latin and Greek, I will no longer be the prey...."
This is how he expressed his relief in a letter to Zola, who had already departed for Paris.

Reading this doggerel, who would guess that Paul Cézanne would become one of the most important painters in the history of art? No one, and since the great transformation that would occur still hung in the balances, his life was something like a soap opera. His father had not changed his mind—his son would become a banker. For that, Paul had to study law. Unable to stand up to his papa, the young Paul could only obey.

"Alas! For Law I took the winding way.
I took—that is not the word, I was forced to take!
Law, terrible law of tangled equivocations,
Which will render my existence frightful for three years!"

Right from the start, law school proved a huge bore. Fortunately, at eighteen Paul had started to go to an open drawing class where he acquired a certain know how, if not a sure knowledge. Put otherwise, although his paintings weren't pleasing, they were already quite strong in their own way. Srong enough that his father didn't stand in his way. In 1860, Paul was finally allowed to go to Paris to enter the competition for a place at the Beaux-Arts. He was certain that everything would go well, but it didn't, and he was deeply disappointed. Feeling discouraged, he returned to Aix to work in his father's bank. He managed for a year, during which time his friend Emile kept pushing for him to come to Paris. Finally, when the year was up, Paul went.

Fortunately, his father didn't fly into a rage and disown him. Paul even received some money in support, but very little. In fact, scarcely enough to survive: "*My good family, excellent in many respects, is perhaps a bit miserly when it comes to an unhappy painter who has never known how to do anything. It's a slight eccentricity, doubtlessly completely forgivable in Provence.*" Polite as always, the young Paul clearly knew how to restrain himself.

Thus it was that he embarked on the hard life of a painter—a life marked by despair, doubts, rejections and many disappointments. (In 1886, he even broke with his dear Zola, believing Zola to have depicted him as a failed painter in one of his novels.) Despite the ups and downs of hard times, Paul never knew the madness of true despair. He was saved by eventual success, recognition and glory, at which he arrived through incredible obstinacy and the remarkable abilities of his hand and eye.

But that's another story – the one of adulthood.

Seeing in harmony.
The Impressionist painters, including Claude Monet who painted the famous, *Impression Soleil Levant*, had a great influence on Cézanne. The Impressionists left their studios to paint out of doors (this in turn led to the invention of paint in tubes.) They depicted reality not as one learns about it in school, but as they saw it, with its changing light and colors over the passage of time. Inspired by this, Cézanne went even further, deforming things to render them as he saw them. He thus broke with the laws of perspective for representing ordinary colored objects, such as apples. His amplified volumes, along with the poses of his nudes, such as *A Modern Olympia*, created a scandal, as did his landscapes, which he painted as if they were mosaics made of stones. Using his small daubs of paint, he painted, for example, many versions of the mountain Sainte-Victoire, which dominated the town of his childhood.

Detail from Apples and Biscuits

CHARLIE CHAPLIN

Charlie Chaplin was born in a poor corner of London on April 16, 1889. His parents, Hannah and Charles, were vaudevillians who formed a comic duo. Off stage, however, they had little to laugh about. Charles was an alcoholic who had no compunction about leaving Hannah only a year after Charlie was born to go to New York to perform. He returned to London, but not to his family. Hannah thus had to support her children (Charlie and his half-brother Sidney) on her own. As a decently-paid performer, she managed for the first five years of Charlie's life, after which her fortunes changed.

During those early years, Charlie and his brother were happy enough. While their mother performed on stage, they did magic tricks, with Charlie (four years younger than Sidney) trying to copy all of his brother's tricks. As a result, one day Charlie "...*swallowed a halfpenny and Mother was obliged to call for a doctor.*" Such was life as a kid in the wings.

When Charlie was five, his mother lost her voice from too many colds and untreated laryngitis. She nevertheless continued to perform to support her family. One evening, her voice cracked and fell to a whisper. The audience began to laugh and catcall. To keep the show going, the stage manager rushed Charlie on stage to replace his mom. Since he had learned to sing and dance almost from the moment he was born, the audience was charmed and showered coins upon him. For Hannah, however, the theater was finished. "*That night was my first appearance on the stage and Mother's last.*" To make ends meet, she took sewing jobs, but the work wasn't enough. Suddenly life became not only hard, but miserable. "*More than once, we had to load our two mattresses, three straw chairs, and meager bundles of clothes onto a cart to move....*"

CHARLIE CHAPLIN (1889-1977), English,
acted in, directed, scripted, produced and
eventually scored his own films. An icon of the silent
film era, he created the character of The Tramp, who
appears in The Kid (1921), The Gold Rush (1925),
Modern Times (1936), and The Great Dictator
(1940). Chaplin made audiences laugh through World
War I, the Great Depression, and World War II.

The Tramp is born one afternoon in 1914. The filming of *Kid Auto Races at Venice* was about to begin. Chaplin was ready, but he didn't yet have his costume or his character. As it happened, Chaplin's Tramp first appeared in this film. Told to pull a comic character together, Chaplin gathered the accessories for his famous silhouette in the blink of an eye. His idea—to play on oppositions. *"I wanted everything a contradiction: the pants baggy, the coat tight, the hat small and the shoes large…. I had no idea of the character. But the moment I was dressed, the clothes and the make-up made me feel the person he was. I began to know him, and by the time I walked onto the stage he was fully born."* Two twirls of his cane, a mustache, and the character existed. *"You know this fellow is many-sided, a tramp, a gentleman, a poet, a dreamer, a lonely fellow, always hopeful of romance and adventure. He would have you believe he is a scientist, a musician, a duke, a polo player. However, he is not above picking up cigarette butts or robbing a baby of its candy."*

A still from the film, 1 A.M.

They were so poor that the boys couldn't even go regularly to school, and when they did they were teased about their clothes, which had been made from their mother's old costumes. Nonetheless, they were well looked after. *"But Mother always stood outside her environment and kept an alert ear for the way we talked, correcting our grammar and making us feel that we were distinguished."*

As they sank into poverty, Hannah began to succumb to mental illness. Finally, without any other recourse, the three of them entered the Lambeth workhouse. There, Hannah was separated from her boys, who soon were transferred to the Hanwell School for Orphans and Destitute Children. Of Hanwell, Charlie recalls, *"I started schooling [there] and was taught to write my name—'Chaplin'. The word fascinated me and looked like me, I thought."*

From there, Sidney went to the Exmouth training ship to be prepared for a life in the Navy. Barely seven years old, Charlie found himself alone. At Hanwell, discipline was strict, and Charlie had to endure the famous physical punishments of British education. Fortunately, Charlie was able to say goodbye to orphanage life when he was nine. Sidney had returned to London and Hannah was able to take her boys back. *"We lived in a miserable room. Most often we had nothing to eat. We didn't have shoes. At times, my mother would take off her boots and one of us would wear them to go to the soup kitchen and bring back our only meal of the day."* Shortly thereafter, Hannah had another breakdown and had to return to the asylum. After a time, she came out, but then had to go in again. When she was out between bouts, she concerned herself with her sons' education, and when possible, they went to school. Charlie found school *"a bleak divertissement, for the presence of other children made me feel less lonely."* Charlie was rather less interested in his classes. History was no more than "*a record of wickedness and violence, a continual succession of regicides and of kings murdering their wives, brothers and nephews; poetry nothing more than exercising memory. Education bewildered me with knowledge and facts in which I was only mildly interested.*"

Fate, however, was on the move. One day during recess, Charlie recited to another boy *Miss Priscilla's Cat*, a small comic piece that his mother had taught him. "*Mr. Reid, our schoolteacher, looked up from his work and was so amused that when the class assembled he made me recite it to them and they were thrown into gales of laughter. As a result of this my fame spread, and the following day I was brought before every classroom in the school, both boys and girls, and made to recite it. Although I had performed and deputized for Mother in front of an audience at the age of five, this was actually my first conscious taste of glamour. School became exciting.*"

Charlie Chaplin was nine years old. He and his brother were nearly destitute and their mother was losing her mind. The future didn't appear happy. Moreover, poor Charlie had developed asthma after a stint with the Eight Lancashire Lads, a troupe of clog dancers. He certainly had no idea that in just a few years he would join a traveling theater troupe in which he would meet incredible actors. Nor did he know that he would read Charles Dickens (this proved significant), the immortal author of *Oliver Twist*, who had the uncanny ability to uncover the ray of light shinning through misery, sickness and solitude. Charlie didn't yet know that he would become The Tramp, as well as perhaps the greatest comic actor of the 20th century.

Yes, now you can smile.

The Great Dictator: **The importance of a mustache.** 1940 saw the release of the film, *The Great Dictator*, a film in which Chaplin gives Hitler (renamed, Hynkel) the traits of his Tramp. As Chaplin tells it, Michael Korda suggested the idea for the film to him in 1937: "*As Hitler had the same mustache as The Tramp, I could play both characters.*" The dangerous rise to power of Nazi Germany decided Chaplin on the film and incited him to take the audacious step of laughing at the dictator. The plot of the film is simple: after many twists and turns, a small time Jewish barber is mistaken for Hynkel and thus begins to upset all that Hynkel has done. After the war, Chaplin had this to say: "*Had I known of the actual horrors of the German concentration camps, I could not have made* The Great Dictator*; I could not have made fun of the homicidal insanity of the Nazis.*"

The Dictator

CHARLEMAGNE

"**W**ho had the mad idea of inventing school one day? It was Charlemagne, bloody Charlemagne!" So the song goes, or at least the one they sing in France. It's true, but there's more to the story than that.

Charles, born in 742, was the son of the king of the Franks, Pippin the Short, and Berthe Big Foot (also known as Queen Goose Foot). As his parents weren't married at the time of his birth, he was considered illegitimate, and hence not destined to rule. Consequently, nobody paid much attention to him. It was just the opposite for his brother, Carloman, who was pampered and educated like a prince. You see, in between the two births, a priest had married Pippin and Berthe.

This fact determined only a small part of Charlie's life, but it certainly was the reason why he was barely educated and spoke only his mother tongue, which is thought to have been "Riparian French," a sort of German, though this is a matter of controversy.

Charlemagne's education was thus rudimentary, except in sports at which he excelled, above all at swimming. It

Charlemagne, king of the Francs in 768, became emperor of the West through his conquests. Around the year 800, with the blessings of the Pope, he became the first ruler since the Romans to reign over a large part of the European continent, raising him above the kings. Once or twice a year, he brought together the powerful of his realm to approve the laws that he wished to promulgate. To assure good governance, the emperor divided them into counts ruled by counts. These upheld his decisions, and in return, they received land for their loyalty. Nevertheless, to keep them in check, Charlemagne relied on inspectors, his famous *missi dominici* (literally, "envoys from the master"), who served to remind people that he was the supreme ruler.

CHARLEMAGNE (742-814),
French-German emperor, whose extensive territories spanned the continent and whose rule was so widespread and culturally rich that he often is considered, "the grandfather of Europe."

Although others before Charlemagne had the idea of inventing school, it was Charlemagne who took the step of expanding educational establishments in episcopates and monasteries, open to boys only. (Not exactly enlightened? Well...no kidding.) Before him, churchmen were just about the only ones who knew how to read, write, do sums, and thus had the ability to teach. In order to oversee his gigantic realm, Charlemagne had need of a greater number of educated men, capable of carrying out his orders and laws. He needed "bureaucrats" who knew how to read.

Mémorables passages des Alpes-2. *Charlemagne, 800.*

Véritable Extrait de Viande LIEBIG.

was only as an adult that he sought to become better educated. As a youth, he read very little, and even as a grown up, he never succeeded in writing properly. "*He always put his writing parchments under his bed pillow so that he might use his moments of leisure to practice his handwriting. However, he had learned his letters too late, and consequently his progress was indifferent.*" So declared Einhard, one of his teachers and a great intellectual of the court, with whom Charles grew up. As for Carloman, he grew into a well-educated and arrogant young man. When father Pippin died and his kingdom was divided between the brothers, the outlying areas went to Charles, while Carloman received the lion's share. As luck would have it, however, Carloman died young and all of his land went to the charismatic Charlie.

Robust, jovial, intelligent, active, courageous and authoritarian—a colorful mix of soldier and peasant—Charlemagne easily won the love of his people. In his court, he surrounded himself with cultivated individuals. "*During meals, he would have stories or chronicles of past times recited aloud or read.*" Among his scholars there was one, Alcuin of York, who was a real mover and shaker. On meeting Alcuin, Charlie knew that he alone could help him achieve a renaissance of learning. Little by little, their conversations turned into tutorials on rhetoric, dialectic and astronomy. Charlemagne proved an excellent student. He understood Greek "*better than he could pronounce it,*" he learned to read Latin, and he became interested in grammar, theology, calculus and philosophy.

The future emperor "*with flowing beard*" (in actuality he wore a moustache in the fashion of the day) clearly understood that instruction was key in assuring his power over his immense realm. He summoned the literate of the land in order to create the Palace School (a sort of super university), and he committed himself to opening schools not just in cities, but in towns and villages as well.

Students from all walks of life were welcome at the Palace School, whether they were rich or poor, noble or not. The only requirement was to possess intellectual and spiritual virtues since the professors were Abbots and Bishops. In other words, to be admitted, one had to be among the best. On this point, Charlemagne was unwavering, for what he was doing, in effect, was recruiting the future cadres of his empire.

No dummy that Charlemagne.

Since the educated people of his day wrote in their own style, which made writing difficult to read, Charlemagne decided to reform the style of writing itself. He universally imposed a form called "Carolingian," which not only is elegant and readable, but also serves as the basis of our own way of writing.

If you happen to have handwriting that's the least bit graceful, you might consider that Charlie the Great is somewhat to thank. We might also thank him for the Carolingian Renaissance, which he helped to foster by protecting the monasteries; giving precedence to theology and the study of religious texts; and increasing the number of art and architecture studios throughout his lands.

What a guy!

Epochal impressions.
In the Middle Ages, printing didn't exist, so it was the monks who reproduced texts by hand on parchments made from animal hides. As the monks used irregular capitals, these texts are now difficult to read. Moreover, with each act of deciphering and recopying, the monk scribes had many opportunities to make mistakes. Carried over from parchment to parchment, their errors multiplied. For this reason, the emperor encouraged the monks to write in lower-case letters called, "Carolingian Miniscule," which over time became the lower-case letters of today. The monks accepted this change, while preserving their habit of inscribing impressions and commentaries in the margins of the texts they were copying: *"How cold it is here…" "I'm hungry, lunchtime make haste." "How annoying this text is!"* Such were the stray thoughts of the scribes as they copied away.

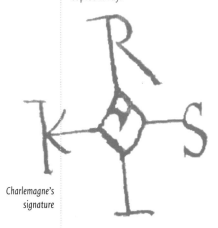

Charlemagne's signature

AGATHA CHRISTIE

Her given name was much more British: Agatha Clarissa Miller. Christie was the name of her first husband, with whom she fell in love at twenty-two. They met at a ball, as in a romance novel, and married two years later.

The queen of mystery was born in 1890 in Torquay, Devonshire. Her father, Frederick (born in America but half British), was a property holder of independent means. Her mother, Clara, was an intellectual and free-thinker who held some radical ideas about child rearing by the time Agatha was born. "*My mother, who had been passionately for education for girls, had now, characteristically, swung round to the opposite view. No child ought to be allowed to read until he was eight years old: better for the eyes and also for the brain.*" Consequently, Agatha's parents oversaw her education, which worked out, since Agatha was fearful and timid. "*[My] games were all make believe. From as early as I can remember, I had various companions of my own choosing.*"

When Agatha was five, her father, beset by money problems, took the family to France for a long vacation because it was cheap. The idea was for Agatha to run around and play outside. But Frederick and Clara, who were rather introspective, left the door to the library open. What a drama! Having poured over picture books, Agatha was already drawn to reading. Her nanny, Nursie, conveyed the news to Clara apologetically: "*I fear, Ma'am...Miss Agatha can **read**.*" So much for Clara's pedagogical theories! Around this time, Agatha also learned French from Marie Sijé, a young French woman. What this meant, of course, was that before long Agatha could read in two languages. Nonetheless, she was still far from being perceived as gifted. "*I myself was always recognized, though quite kindly, as the 'slow one' of the family. The reactions of my mother*"

AGATHA CHRISTIE (1890-1976),
British mystery writer, most known for her
books, Murder on the Orient Express, Ten
Little Indians, and Death on the Nile. Her
complete oeuvre includes more than eighty
titles that have been translated and read
throughout the world. Her less famous autobiography is a wonderful book in its own right.

The Detective novel relates facts that follow from a crime. It's various plots are based on suspense and involve the reader in a pursuit or investigation. Among the "godfathers" of the genre, which appeared in the nineteenth century, the names that stand out are Edgar Allan Poe (1809-1849), Conan Doyle (1859-1930), the father of Sherlock Holmes, and Agatha Christie, often regarded as their heiress. Above all, she contributed to establishing the rules for the "classic" detective novel. Her detectives, Hercule Poirot and Miss Marple, solve mysteries thanks to their incomparable reasoning and their knowledge of the human mind. In her books, murder and investigation often unfold in close proximity.

Excavations at the foot of the Giza Sphinx in Egypt.

and my sister were unusually quick—I could never keep up. I was, too, very inarticulate. ... 'Agatha's so terribly slow,' was always the cry."

Not surprisingly, Agatha's mother was a devoted reader who also liked to write. She entertained writers at home, such as Rudyard Kipling (of *Jungle Book* fame), and encouraged her daughters to write. Madge, Agatha's older sister, was published in the ultra chic, *Vanity Fair*. It wasn't until Agatha was about twenty that she tried her hand at writing while recovering from influenza. "Why don't you write a story?" Mother suggested. "Write a story?" I said, rather startled. "Yes," said Mother. "Like Madge." "Oh, I don't think I could." The title of her first serious effort (she had written many things as a child) was *The House of Beauty*.

But to go back... It was when Agatha was eleven that her father died and the sky over her childhood darkened. A year later her sister married and her brother, the officer, left for India. Agatha became the only child at home. "I stepped out of my child's world, a world of security and thoughtlessness, to enter the fringes of the world of reality."

Having believed that the best education for Agatha was out of doors, Agatha's mother now sent her to Miss Guyer's very select finishing school. Next, she took Agatha to Paris and enrolled her in another select school to perfect her French and refine her style. At sixteen, Agatha spent most of her time playing the piano and singing. She became quite good, but sadly the poor girl had stage fright. Having devoted herself to music for two years, she had to give it up because of her inability to perform. "[This] taught me that I had not the kind of temperament for exhibition of any kind."

For a change her mother took her to Egypt. "I went to five

dances every week. They were given in each of the big hotels in turn." On her return to England, she lived much the same life, and it was at one of the many dances to which she went that she met Archibald Christie, her first husband. She was engaged to another man at the time, but when Archie tracked her down after the dance and proposed, she realized that she was in love. Christie had mystery. Was it the conversation she had had with her sister only a short time before that decided her? *"I said I should like to try my hand at a detective story. 'I don't think you could do it,' said Madge. 'They are very difficult to do, I've thought about it.' 'I should like to try.' 'Well I bet you couldn't,' said Madge. There the matter rested. From that moment I was fired by the determination that I would write a detective story."*

It wasn't until World War I, in which she worked as a nurse before moving to the dispensary, that the idea for her first mystery took shape. It was in the quiet of the dispensary that she began to write. The result: in 1916, at the age of twenty-five, Agatha completed *The Mysterious Affair of Styles*, in which her Belgian detective, Hercule Poirot, first appeared. Her very long list of imperishable masterpieces had begun.

Her secret? Perhaps this comment provides the key. *"One of the luckiest things that can happen to you in life is, I think, to have a happy childhood. I had a very happy childhood. I had a home and a garden that I loved; a wise and patient nanny; as father and mother two people who loved each other dearly and made a success of their marriage and of parenthood."*

Thus she was free as an adult to devote herself to crime and murder.

Interesting, isn't it?

From the movie of Death on the Nile with Peter Ustinov as Hercule Poirot.

Luxurious houses and first-class trains and boats. From one book to another, the reader travels with Agatha Christie, and the characters that the reader accompanies are often the most socially privileged. As for her settings, Christie mostly took them from the trips she made with her second husband, an archeologist, especially to Egypt. Many of her novels were inspired by the events she witnessed in her life: the First and Second World Wars and the Cold War. She also witnessed a revolution in media that only served to increase her fame. Her books have been adapted over and over again for radio, TV and film.

WINSTON CHURCHILL

Churchill was the little roly-poly with a cigar who, without a doubt, saved his country, Europe, and perhaps even the world, through his fierce opposition to Hitler.

Born in 1874, Winston was a beautiful, rosy baby in excellent health. ("*Every baby resembles me!*" he later said to end all discussion of his girth). His only problem as a little lad was, to put it bluntly, his very British aristocratic family, of the sort where parents see their children at a set time to receive reports from the nanny and tutors. His father, Lord Randolph, was a politician. His mother, Jennie, was a vivacious, beautiful American at home in the world of high society. In other words, his childhood was privileged but not entirely happy.

In the closed world where Winston grew up, all male descendants were prepared for admittance to the most elite universities from the age of reason (seven) on. Consequently, the young Winston had to be trained for "the must," namely Eton; however, such preparation comes at a cost, and in this case, it took its toll.

"You chose dishonor and you will have war!" When Hitler took power in Germany in 1933, Churchill was already on his guard. But memories of the First World War were sharp and determining: the British and the French wanted to avoid another conflict at all cost, even if the price to be paid was to let the German dictator seize Central Europe. When Hitler invaded Czechoslovakia, the governments of France and Britain negotiated with him. Strongly opposed to this attitude, Churchill prophesied: "*You were given the choice between war and dishonor. You chose dishonor and you will have war.*"

At eight, Winston was torn from the tender embrace of his nanny, Mrs. Everest, and sent off to the St. James School in Ascot. "*I counted the days and the hours to the end of every term, when I should return home from this hateful servitude and range my soldiers in line of battle on the nursery floor.*" Finding his classes dry and uninteresting, he made little effort. "*Where my reason, imagination or interest were not engaged, I would not or I could not learn.*" Thus he was often punished, even lashed.

"*I fell into a low state of health...and finally after a serious illness my parents took me away. Our family doctor...practiced at*

WINSTON CHURCHILL (1874-1965)
already had a long political career behind him when, named prime minister of England in 1940,
he became the symbol of the resistance of the "free world" to Hitler's Germany.

Brighton; and as I was now supposed to be very delicate, it was thought desirable that I should be under his constant care. I was accordingly, in 1883, transferred to a school at Brighton kept by two ladies." At this small, more easy-going school, he was treated kindly and allowed to study the subjects that interested him: French, history and poetry. As a result, Winston thrived over his three years there.

During this period, Winston also started to read the newspaper in the hope of getting some news of his father. Newspapers and the news thus became a life-long passion.

But neither his improvement at school nor his passion for the press were enough to get him into Harrow, the elite boarding school that traditionally took those who weren't "strong enough" for Eton. When Winston took the entrance exam, he sort of cracked up. *"I wrote my name at the top of the page. I wrote down the number of the question "I". After much reflection I put a bracket round it thus '(I)'. But thereafter I could not think of anything connected with it that was either relevant or true. Incidentally there arrived from nowhere in particular a blot and several smudges. I gazed for two whole hours at this sad spectacle...."*

There was, however, no need to panic. His family name was fashionable enough to open the doors to Harrow nonetheless.

Once there, he continued to dream, and his god was the poet Byron. When he wasn't dreaming, he was, well, rebelling. His mother received a letter concerning—Heavens!—*"tardiness, the loss of books and phenomenal negligence."* His father, the lord, wrote to his son, *"Your schoolwork is an insult to your intelligence."* Did he really mean to Winston's, or was it perhaps his own pride that he had in mind? We'll never know. However, to end all of the argu-

Fighting for a cause within a storm. On September 3, 1939, England and France no longer had a choice: Germany had attacked their ally, Poland, and they had to declare war. With this declaration, the Second World War, which would leave 50 million dead, had begun. The European countries had already endured nine months of terrible upheaval and doubt when, in May 1940, Winston Churchill was named prime minister. Posing Britain as the *"bulwark of the free world,"* Churchill declared his willingness to fight unto victory, but all he could promise was *"blood, suffering, tears, and sweat."* All the same he said a lot, and what he said counted. As President Kennedy declared in 1963, *"He mobilized the English language and he sent it into battle."*

ments, his father craftily suggested that perhaps Winston, who was about to turn fifteen, would like to be trained for the military. Winston was delighted! Nevertheless, it took him three attempts to pass the entrance exams to Sandhurst, the best military school in Britain, and even then he entered at the lowest possible level. Of 389 candidates, he was nearly last on his first attempt; on his second, he was 203rd; finally, he ranked 95th and was admitted. His military education had begun!

When his father died of illness, leaving the family on the verge of ruin, Winston was left to support himself. He decided that he would go into politics. His mother, who still had ties to powerful circles, promised to help him as much as possible. But first, Winston had to make his way in the cavalry.

As the British were everywhere in the world at the time, Winston first went to India, where he was bored and devoured *The Life of Celebrated Men* as recounted by an old Roman. Next he went to Egypt, the Sudan, and South Africa, where the Boers, the descendents of Dutch colonists, were trying to throw the Brits out. Taking advantage of this experience, Winston wrote several articles and a book, which had a degree of success despite its faults.

In 1900 at the age of twenty-six, Churchill was elected to the parliament. Later he would say, "*Success is the ability to go from failure to failure without losing your enthusiasm.*" True enough. Despite the many setbacks in the war against Hitler, it was his unflagging commitment and determination that led to the first major defeat of Germany and kept German forces from British soil.

Now that's enthusiasm!

London after a bombing

The Battle of Britain.
German troops marched down the Champs-Élysée in Paris in June 1940. They already had occupied Belgium and The Netherlands and were now dangerously close to the shores of England. Under Churchill's leadership, England did not surrender even after months of bombings by the Germans. This was the first setback for an undefeated Germany. After the bombings, which caused terrible fires, the prime minister appeared in the ravaged streets of London. From the Battle of Britain (so-named by Churchill in his "Finest Hour" speech) of June through October 1940, to the bloody D-Day landing of 1944, Churchill led the way to victory. In February 1945, with Franklin D. Roosevelt and Joseph Stalin, he participated in the Yalta Conference, where, as the well-known saying goes, the three major powers "*divided the world.*" In July of the same year, Churchill was not reelected, largely because the British wanted to forget the war.

Leonardo Da Vinci

I, Leonardo, forewarn you that I am an F.U.G. (future universal genius). No, I am not of noble birth. Vinci is just the name of the town where I was born in 1452. My mother, Caterina, was a peasant who couldn't resist a more prosperous notary. Right from the start, then, this F.U.G. was an illegitimate child, who would know neither his mother nor his father very well. Seemingly that didn't pose a problem in my corner of Italy at the time I was born. I say "seemingly" because I don't remember much of anything about it. I therefore have to rely on a terrible painter of my epoch named Vasari, who became famous for recounting the lives of the artists of his time. But again, be forewarned: Vasari, who often said no matter what, should not be trusted.

As a child, I went back and forth between the country, which I adored and where I loved to observe tiny particles of dew, and the town where my paternal grandparents introduced me to the potter's art. Yes, this F.U.G. started with vases and cooking pots. Or, at least, that's what Vasari wrote. What I do recall is that I was often free and left to my own devices, and thus I had to learn to write all by myself. So what I did with my right hand was to begin on the right-hand side of the page. I also spent time with my uncle, Francesco, tending animals, exploring and observing the landscape that I would later draw. When my grandfather died, my old man, Ser Piero, took me in. As it turned out, he spent much of his time getting married. (As for myself, I never married.) Wishing to make a small banker of me (in Italy at the time there were many of those), he had me learn arithmetic. As Vasari described it, *"after several months of mathematics, he had made so much progress that he often embarrassed his teacher by relentlessly asking*

LEONARDO DA VINCI (1452-1519), Italian painter, inventor, military engineer, scientist, writer, and court artist in both Italy and France. The range of his knowledge and the extent of his talents have led him to be called the genius of the Renaissance.

Vasari's bet.
Vasari was born at the
beginning of the 16th century, in
1511, eight years before Leonardo
died. They therefore did not know
each other. The two men, originally from Tuscany, a region in the
center of Italy, had something of
the same background. Vasari also
knew poetry and literature well
and was almost apprenticed to a
glass blower before being accepted
into the studio of the famous
Michelangelo. Vasari eventually
became the head of a studio, overseeing more than twenty appren-
tices. Paralleling his activities as a
painter, he began to write his *Lives
of the Artists*, which took sixteen
years. His goal: to bear witness to
the great masters of his time as
well as of two centuries before, so
that the men of the future would
not forget them. Vasari won his
wager since today we still read
him, sometimes to critique his
work, but mostly to find out about
the artists and artworks of the
Renaissance.

difficult questions." Vasari also depicted me as capricious
and easily distracted: *"...he undertook research in different
areas and once having begun, he would abandon it."* Evidently
this idiot didn't realize that I was simply curious and hungry for the new. The proof of this: I read constantly. That's
just how I was made. It's my nature to be interested in
everything: art, music, poetry, and, of course, the drawing
that I did just like that without having learned anything at
all.

Impressed by my efforts, my father showed several of
them to the great master Verrocchio, who was even more
amazed and immediately agreed to take me on. A real
fairytale, but only in the abstract, as you will see. This was
because in a Florentine studio of the time, an apprentice
had to start at the bottom—washing paint brushes, prim-
ing surfaces, preparing paints, sweeping up, running to
fetch beer, and the like, before being allowed to paint the
small bits that the master might toss him.

That, however, was completely agreeable to me. I flour-
ished, exploring everything and inventing. It was a real party.

When Verrocchio had to deliver a *Baptism of Christ*, he
finally offered two of his students, Botticelli and me, the
chance to work on it. It would seem that he was over-
whelmed by the perfection of the angel that I quickly did
for him. As Vasari wrote, *"Following this, humiliated to see
that a child knew more than he, [Verrocchio] never again wanted
to touch a paintbrush."* He's not entirely wrong here, which
is fine, but let's move on. Instead of continuously painting the same theme like Botticelli, who made *"truly sad
landscapes,"* I observed and experimented. I explored
plants, flowers, and trees as well as the heavens. I also

drew the bones, muscles and organs of humans as well as animals. I liked to dream because, "*in infinity, the spirit awakens to new inventions.*" I enrolled in the guild of Florentine painters, and a year later, I painted my first great canvas, *The Landscape of Santa Maria della Neve*. It was said that its light surpassed all of what had been done up to that time, but once again it was Vasari who said that.

In so far as I was an F.U.G., it wasn't necessary to shy away from anything. Thus I studied perspective, geometry, and all that I could know of the sciences of my epoch. I also read all of the time, moving from hydraulics to anatomy, optics, studies of bird flight, mathematics, and ballistics. What Vasari neglects to mention is that I also learned the best way to bake a pizza.

All the same, my extensive research didn't keep the Pope from inviting Botticelli (him again!) and his colleagues to the Vatican, but not me. Furious, I sent my resumé to Ludovic Sforza the Moor, duke of Milan. Given the list of my competencies, despite their disorganized presentation, the duke engaged me. Not as an artist, but as an engineer. My job was to find a way to build tanks, fortifications and a whole stock of machines. He counted upon me equally to organize and design his wild parties and festivals, and so I became, as you say today, his CCO (Chief Communications Officer).

I was described by a witness of my times as, "*an admirable inventor, an arbitrator of all of the refinements, above all of the pleasures of the theater, singing knowingly and accompanying himself on the lyre, appreciated and loved to the highest degree by all of the princes who know him.*" Ludovic the Moor even told me, "*If your body were equal to your spirit, you would not be of*

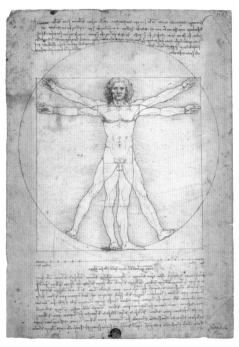

Man, the measure of all things

The Renaissance

The 15th century, the century of Leonardo, marked the end of the long Middle Ages and the beginning of a new period, known as the Renaissance. It was in Italy, the richest country in Europe, that it first began. Philosophical and scientific texts from Antiquity were rediscovered. The Italian artists and scientists who read them were inspired to rethink the place of human beings in the world. They also endeavored to understand the past as well as the workings of the body and the mind. Thanks to the books that multiplied and circulated with the invention of the printing press (the middle of the 15th century), their questions and ways of seeing spread throughout Europe. Before too long, with the discovery of America, Europe would once again extend the limits of the known world.

From the anonymous medieval artisan to the stars of the Renaissance. The change in the way artists were viewed is a striking example of the changes brought by the Renaissance. Throughout the Middle Ages, artists were looked upon as artisans who executed work orders. In other words, it was the skill of these craftsmen that enabled them to take on commissions and fulfill them. With the Renaissance, however, artists began to be seen as unique individuals, each endowed with individual qualities and talents. Artists began to sign their works, and those who were deemed most talented by the brokers of culture became the stars.

this world. *Your fame spreads like bread in the hands of children.*" All the same, I was handsome! And above all, I enjoyed myself. Everybody, men and women, came my way. I even put on burlesque farces to laugh at myself. I also got back at the scholars who criticized me for not making a distinction between literature, painting and mechanics. "*Everything is science and practice issues from knowledge.*" With that, I dealt them a blow, even when it came to painting, because I always painted, albeit slowly.

The critics whined a bit because of my delays (too much work! My record: twenty-five years for *The Virgin of the Rocks*), or when I didn't completely finish a painting, *The Adoration*, for example. But I also had a theory about that. An unfinished canvas was better, and it was fashionable. At the time, that even had a name: the "*non-finito.*" Not to finish was a way of saying that one should not approach perfection, with that reserved for the Creator alone. But hold on! That said, when I finished *The Last Supper* admiration was universal. Sadly, this fresco fell into ruin too quickly because I used tons of non-standard products when painting it.

When Milan, where I lived, went to war with France, I endured periods of boredom. For example, I had prepared everything to make a magnificent equestrian statue for the duke, but the bronze had to be melted down to make cannons. In 1499 I had to leave Milan because my dear Ludovic the Moor had been beaten. Suddenly I was obliged to sell my advice and services to Florence and Venice, as well as to the Vatican, which I did for the next sixteen years. I even drew geographical maps. It was during this time that I presented my *Mona Lisa*, the most famous painting in the world. Nevertheless my existence remained uncertain, and I had to look for work everywhere. I even proposed the construction of a bridge over the Bosphorus to Bajazet, the Turkish sultan, but he was too arrogant to deign to reply. Thus, in 1516, when François I proposed to bring me to France, I accepted. In any case, I already had passed from the stage of F.U.G. to that of U.G.: universal genius. I was curious, universally curious! That's really what the Renaissance was about, curiosity on a grand scale. In fact, that's what genius also is—unending, unstoppable curiosity.

In Amboise, near the royal chateau, François I gave me a house and a lavish stipend of 2,000 écus, a fortune. His only requirement was for me to continue my research in peace for a couple of years. Ah, France! The salaries! And the security of employment!

But let's not forget the good Vasari, since he also wrote, "*The most heavenly gifts seem to be showered on certain human beings. Sometimes supernaturally, marvelously, they all congregate in one individual.... This was seen and acknowledged by all men in the case of Leonardo da Vinci.*"

What a guy! Thank goodness he wasn't a better painter.

The Mona Lisa

SALVADOR DALI

Salvador Felipe Jacinto, the greatest cosmic and paranoid genius in the universe, was born in Figueras, a small town in Catalonia, Spain, on May 11, 1904.

"My parents baptized me Salvador, like my brother. As my name indicates, I was destined for nothing less than to rescue painting from the void of modern art, and this at an epoch of catastrophes, in the mechanical and mediocre universe where we have the distress and the honor of living."

A savior? Hmm, but what's really curious is that Salvador was given the name of his dead brother. By the time he was five, the poor boy understood that his parents saw him as nothing less than his brother's reincarnation. "His death plunged my mother and father into the depths of despair; they found consolation only upon my arrival in the world. My brother and I resembled each other like two drops of water, but we had different reflections. Like myself he had the unmistakable facial morphology of a genius. He gave signs of alarming precocity, but his glance was veiled by the melancholy characterizing insurmountable intelligence. I, on the other hand, was much less intelligent, but I reflected everything. " Ole!

His parents spoke French and moved in the fashionable world of art. His father was authoritarian in style, but Dali wasn't traumatized in the least. "I wet my bed till the age of eight for the sheer fun of it. Nothing was good enough for me. My father and mother worshipped me." Ole again!

"At the age of six I wanted to be a cook. At seven I wanted to be Napoleon," he declared as an adult. School, however, was another story. Even though he learned French at the young age of six, this "genius" did not shine at school. Already fascinated by forms and images, he had better things to do than his schoolwork. Instead, he drew and painted. In the studio he set up, he gave himself over to his imagination. "In the course of my interminable and exhausting reveries,

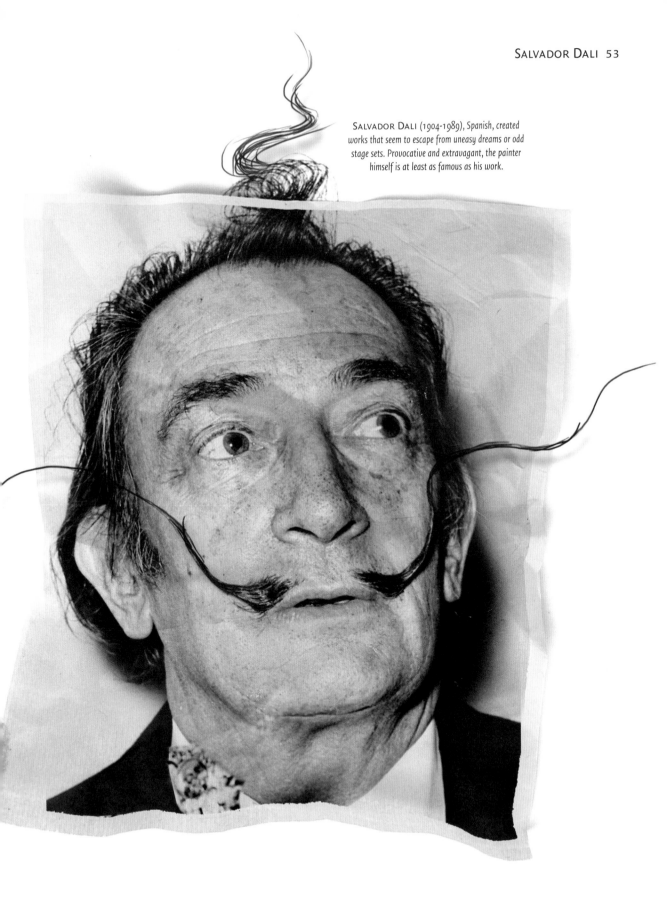

SALVADOR DALI (1904-1989), Spanish, created works that seem to escape from uneasy dreams or odd stage sets. Provocative and extravagant, the painter himself is at least as famous as his work.

Beyond prudent appearances.
At one point, Dali belonged to
the Surrealist movement. The
Surrealists, headed by the French
writer André Breton, thought that
it was necessary to free oneself
from reason and logic in order to
create. For them, remembering
dreams was an essential source of
inspiration. It was at this time that
Dali worked with Bunuel on the
films *Chien Andalou* and *L'age d'or*,
both of which defied good taste and
the morality of the church. The
screening of *L'age d'or* in Paris in
1930 created a scandal. Protestors
threw smoke and stink bombs to
drive the spectators from the cinema, and they waited with bludg-
eons at the exits. The paintings of
Max Ernst, Dali, and Miro, exhibited for the occasion, were slashed.
The outcome was that the police
prohibited the film. Following this,
Dali argued with Breton, who gave
him the nickname, "Avida Dollars"
an anagram that played on Dali's
taste for fashionable society and
money.

*Dali's lobster
telephone*

my eyes would untiringly follow the vague irregularities of these
moldy silhouettes and I saw rising from this chaos which was as
formless as clouds progressively more concrete images which by
degrees became endowed with an increasingly precise, detailed and
realistic personality."* This is how it also was when he went on
vacation to the beach in Cadaques, a small fishing village,
where the rocks of the coast were an invitation to dream.

In contrast, Salvador was fast, almost frantic, when he
painted. Enrolled at twelve in the municipal drawing
school, he participated in his first exhibition at fifteen. By
sixteen, he freely declared that he would live by his talent
alone. From that time on, Dali gave himself the appearance
of an artist. *"I let my hair grow like that of a young girl and, in
contemplating myself before the mirror, I liked to adopt the melancholy stance and gaze of Raphael in his self-portrait...."* Ole!
As his paintings had already started to be noticed, his
father decided to send him to the prestigious Academy of
Fine Arts in Madrid, where he was admitted at seventeen.
His mother died the same year.

The young Salvador quickly became part of the Spanish
avant-garde. During the 1920s, there were in that group
those who would become venerable old dogs, such as
Louis Bunuel, the filmmaker, and Garcia Lorca, the poet.
Dali remained friends with them for a long time, though
eventually his energies were spent in getting angry at
them. During this period Salvador developed opinionated
and vaguely revolutionary political ideas. Without warning, though unsurprisingly, he was suspended from the
Academy for a year. On returning to Figueras, he was
imprisoned by the Civil Guard, no doubt under pressure
from his irritated father. *"I was always talking about anarchy
and monarchy, deliberately linking them together...."* Released

after a few weeks, he became a local Vedette (mounted sentry). He was twenty.

After a year, he returned to the Academy of Fine Arts, where his hangers-on welcomed him back with relief. "*They were all disoriented, lost and dead of an imaginative famine that I alone was capable of placating. I was acclaimed, I was looked after, I was coddled. I became their divinity.*" Though rebellious, Salvador still produced a lot of work and exhibited. In 1926, he went to Paris for the first time, where he met Picasso and visited the Louvre. He also crossed over to The Netherlands, where he discovered Vermeer and Bosch. On his return to Spain, he was kicked out of the Academy of Fine Arts for good. Having refused to take exams because he knew more than his professors, the jury declared him "*incompetent.*" At that he could only laugh, while painting ever more astonishing subjects, such as rotten donkeys and cut-off hands.

In 1928, Salvador returned to Paris where things began to heat up. There he fell in with the Surrealists André Breton, Man Ray, René Magritte, and Tristan Tzara. He collaborated with Bunuel on the films *Chien Andalou* and *L'age d'or*, which created a scandal and made him even more famous. He found patrons, a huge step, and met the poet, Paul Eluard, whose wife, Gala, he met a year later in Cadaques. Falling madly in love, he carried her away like a real Romeo, but only after she had moved from repulsion to desire. 1929 was thus the year that Salvador came into his own: 1. Gala 2. His acclaimed painting, *The First Days of Spring*.

Even if over his immense career, Dali offered everything and its opposite, playing the clown, the genius, the idiot, the mystic, the philosopher, and a downright nuisance, he still remained faithful to Gala and art. Ole!

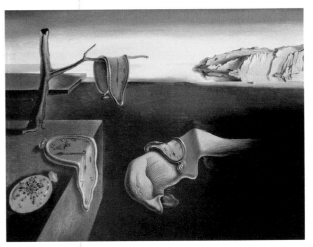

The Persistence of Memory
Of his painting *The Persistence of Memory*, popularly known as *The Melting Clocks*, Dali said, "You can be sure that my famous soft watches are nothing other than the affectionate, extravagant, lonely, paranoid-critical Camembert of time and space."

CHARLES DARWIN

Global travel.

In his work, Darwin relied on what he had seen during the expedition of the *Beagle* and on his readings. He knew by heart the 36 volumes of the German explorer von Humboldt, who had written about his travels in North America. Darwin also had read the work of Lamarck, who coined the word, "*biology*." It is thanks to Lamarck that he became convinced that the earth and its species evolved "peacefully." Darwin verified this thesis in South America when he unearthed fossils and skeletons of prehistoric animals from deep in the ground. At the time, many thought that these remains proved that catastrophes, such as the Flood recounted in the Bible, had violently caused the disappearance of many species from the earth.

Humans descend from monkeys. This is what Darwin is taken to have demonstrated, but it's not exactly right: humans and monkeys are really cousins according to his idea, but all right.

As for Darwin, he himself descended from a longish line of doctors and scientists. Born in England in 1809, Charles had no real difficulties (he was simply naughty and lazy like so many kids) until the age of eight, when his mother died. Following that, little Charles went to school, first to a religious institution, then to a boarding school, where his immature behavior led him to be taken for younger than his years. As he later wrote, "*Nothing could have been worse for the development of my mind than Dr. Butler's School, as it was strictly classical.… The school as a means of education to me was simply a blank.*" He showed himself to be a mediocre student, for whom hunting and fishing counted more than Latin, History, and Geography. "*I believe that I was considered a very ordinary boy, rather below the common standard in intellect.*"

He loved vacations best of all. He spent time with his many cousins, studied plants, insects and birds, and collected everything that came into his hands. When he was alone, he read poetry (above all Shakespeare, who descends directly from Greek tragedy), and he explored geometry and experimental chemistry with his brother. In other words, Darwin was a completely ordinary boy (although in relation to the monkey from whom he descended, he was already quite remarkable). "*To my deep mortification my father once said to me, 'you care for nothing but shooting, dogs, and rat-catching, and you will be a disgrace to yourself and your family.'*"

As his father's dearest wish was for him to become a doc-

CHARLES DARWIN (1809-1882),
English naturalist, published On the
Origin of Species by Means of Natural
Selection *in 1859 and* The Descent of
Man *in 1871, wherein he concluded that
humans share the same ancestor with the
monkey. Although the church and many scientists fought against his ideas, his theories
revolutionized the life sciences as well as the
way in which we think about ourselves.*

The finches of the Galapagos and their great-uncle from South America . The *Beagle* put down anchor in the archipelago of the Galapagos Islands, separated one from the other by a distance of about 50 miles. On those islands, Darwin saw giant tortoises and iguanas. He also discovered that each island had its own species of finch and that each had its own characteristic beak, different in size and shape from those of the finches on neighboring islands. Moreover, all of these species could be distinguished from the only type of finch familiar to Darwin, which had appeared in South America much earlier when the Galapagos hadn't even formed yet. Darwin divined that the finches of the Galapagos, taken together, were the heirs of the South American finch. These heirs had adapted to the conditions of life on each of the islands where they found themselves. From a single species, thirteen others had issued, each different from the other.

tor (this trait will not evolve within the family), he entered Edinburgh University at sixteen. Problems arose, however, as he was unable to handle dissections and the insides of the body disgusted him (later in life he regreted not having made more of an effort since the practice would have proved invaluable in his work). Moreover, as he wasn't good at drawing, he found himself poorly adapted to anatomical sketching. Nevertheless, he discovered zoology and read the works of Lamarck with fascination. He also learned to stuff dead birds and delivered a couple of papers to the Plinian Society, which met, "... *for the sake of reading papers on natural science and discussing them. I used regularly to attend, and the meetings had a good effect on me in stimulating my zeal....*"

However, as the sight of blood continued to make Charles squeamish, his stint at Edinburgh U. seemed pointless. "*I...saw two very bad operations, one on a child, but I rushed away before they were completed. Nor did I ever attend again...this being long before the blessed days of chloroform. The two cases fairly haunted me for many a long year.*" He was eighteen years old when he returned home.

Disappointed and worried that Charles would remain idle, his father suggested that he become a clergyman. Charles agreed, thinking this would afford him ample time for his nature walks. Matriculating at Cambridge University, he attempted to overcome his slow start with the help of a tutor. A tough thing to accomplish in only three years.

At Cambridge, no miracles occurred and, except for Euclide's geometry and natural philosophy, his studies failed to inspire him, and he wasted his time in a dissipated, sporting life. Nevertheless, he succeeded in assembling and classifying a great number of beetles of all kinds, a pursuit he followed with great pleasure. Whom else did this interest? Beetle enthusiasts, of course. He also assisted in the classes taught by John Stevens Henslow, a cleric-botanist, with whom Darwin went on long walks. "I was even called 'the man who walks with Henslow'." He also read the travel writings of Alexander von Humboldt with keen interest. Finally, at twenty-two, he received his diploma and became a Bachelor of Arts, 10th in his class out of 178 students. Hats off!

On the heels of this success, Professor Henslow persuaded him to study geology on an excursion into North Wales. Not exactly Peru, but that didn't matter, since Charles learned to do fieldwork and to make out the geology of a region. Next, dear old Henslow recommended Darwin to Captain FitzRoy, who was preparing to leave for South America and sought a young naturalist. The expedition's mission: "to complete the study of the costs of Patagonia and Tierra del Fuego, to map out the coasts of Chile, Peru, and several islands in the Pacific, and finally to make a series of observations around the world."

Catastrophe nearly struck when his father refused to let him go. Fortunately he added a caveat: "If you can find any man of common sense, who advises you to go, I will give my consent." Charles' savior was his good uncle Josiah, who interceded on his behalf, and he was given permission to go. He was still twenty-two. What a year!
Over the course of his five years on the *Beagle*, Darwin discovered seasickness along with the world. He also spent time reflecting deeply on all he saw. So deeply, in fact, that upon his return he established his famous theory of evolution, which still has us reflecting today. Or some of us, anyway, since there still are those who reject his theory.
But that, dear reader, is another story.

Natural Selection: advantage to the lucky ones

The shape of a beak, the thickness of a skin, or the length of a neck can vary over time. What drives this variation, wrote Darwin, is *"natural selection."* Let's say an animal has a nice thick fur: he is better protected against the cold than his "brother" of the same set of offspring. Another example: an animal runs more quickly than his "brother," meaning that he has more of a chance of escaping from enemies. Within each species, those who initially possess these fortunate advantages will prove to be more numerous as adults. They, in turn, will transmit these advantages to their children. These characteristics—*"useful variations"*—are favorable for survival and are reinforced little by little in each species, which thus is transformed over millions of years.

ALEXANDRA DAVID-NÉEL

Lhassa, the capital of Tibet, *was* an independent state until China invaded in 1951, subjecting its population to terrible oppression and coercion. Before this, religious Buddhist monks ruled the country from their ancient palace-monastery in Lhasa. Situated in the Himalayas at an altitude of more than 11,800 feet, at the heart of the highest mountain range in the world, Lhassa was a city forbidden to outsiders. That is all it took for Alexandra to be tempted. After traveling nearly 1,865 miles on foot with her adopted Asian son, she entered the city disguised as a beggar and lived there for two months. What was she after? To study Buddhism up close. *"When I am criticized by the scholars of the Ivory Tower, it must be that the public can think: yes, those people are eminent scholars, but she lived among the things of which she speaks, she touched them and saw them as living ...."*

Born in Paris in 1868 into a socially prominent family, Louise Eugénie Alexandrine Marie didn't know that she would live to be over one hundred and that she, therefore, would have time to fulfill most of her dreams. A writer, opera singer, oriental philosopher, feminist journalist, political anarchist, Buddhism expert, spiritual searcher and fearless explorer, she was extraordinary by any measure. Perhaps most remarkable was her entry into the forbidden city of Lhasa at the age of fifty-five after four months of incredible hardship. The first Westerner to enter the city, she traveled thousands of miles on foot across the Himalayas to get there. Now that's impressive!

Before achieving that, however, she was a child, and so we need to go back a little. As a young child, "Nini," as she was called, was proud, independent, and hungry for freedom. From the very beginning, she seemed to practice the art of flight: *"I learned to run before I could walk!"* At the age of two, she ran away from her parents, *"two statues who never met."*

Her mother had no interest in her. *"She wanted a child to use as a toy, that is all."* Fortunately, Nini admired her erudite father, Louis, a professor and journalist, whom she loved most of all. *"I was so much his daughter, and his daughter alone, that I despised in myself all that might have been transmitted through my maternal heredity."*

At age five, she ran away from home to explore the forest of Vincennes. She was so angry at the policeman who brought her home that she dug her nails into his hand deep enough to draw blood. Around this time, she also taught herself to read and became the sister of a little boy whom she regarded with rage and curiosity. *"Hold on! I*

ALEXANDRA DAVID-NÉEL (1868-1969),
French explorer, popularized Buddhism in the West and recounted her
travels through Asia in over thirty books. In My Journey to Lhasa, she
wrote about her 1924 journey to a city that was forbidden to foreigners.
The manuscripts that she carried out of Tibet, translated and published,
have preserved vital texts (particularly those of the early Buddhist
philosopher Nagarjuna) that otherwise would have been lost.

How Prince Siddhartha became the Enlightened One, the Buddha.
Buddhism wasn't born in Tibet but in the mountains of neighboring India. This is how. It is told that in the sixth century BCE the young Siddhartha ruled over his country without ever having left his sumptuous palace, his beautiful wife, and his children. One morning the prince decided to go beyond his walls. Outside, he successively met a beggar, an old man and a corpse. Full of despair at having discovered poverty, old age and death, Siddhartha questioned himself about the meaning of life. Abandoning everything, he traveled around the world in search of an answer. Filled with knowledge and wisdom by his journey, Siddhartha finally understood that suffering is the only thing shared by all beings. Henceforth called "Buddha," which means Awakened One, Siddhartha preached this idea, while teaching the way to a cessation of suffering. Today Buddhism is practiced by about 6% of the entire world population. Christians make up about 33%, Muslims 21%, Hindus 14%, and Jews .2%.

Tintin, another Tibet ambassador

won't have this!" As it turned out, her brother died shortly after birth, which came as a great relief. *"From now on, everything will be about me."* Clearly she was a strong character even as a child! Her feelings are interesting insofar as it was after her brother's death that she began to think of herself as a boy. That she later fell in love with Pierrot at the Guignol in Paris confused her a little, though not for long, since she was already passionate about Asia, the thought of which absorbed her endlessly. Her passion was such that Nini was convinced that she had Mongolian blood in her veins through her grandmother, who was of Siberian origin. Her father himself was compelled to admit, *"My daughter has white skin, but her soul is yellow."*

When Nini was six, her family moved to Ixelles, south of Brussels in Belgium. It was there that she spent most of her youth, cloistered in the family library, which only enhanced her hunger for flight. It was at school that she discovered her interest in religion, or rather religious beliefs. By the time she was thirteen, Nini wanted to be a missionary so that she could go to the four corners of the earth to speak about God. Thoughts of travel once again.

Her parents, however, were domestic types. Consequently, Alexandra suffocated at home, burdened by a sense of wasted time. *"My parents—like most doting parents who have raised, if not a large eagle, at least a diminutive eaglet obsessed with flying through the air—could not comprehend this in the least and although no worse than others, they did me more harm than a relentless enemy."*

At fifteen, she went to England on her own, passing through The Netherlands, and only returned home after she had spent all she had in her purse. Two years later, she escaped again. Disguised as a woman of means, she took a train through Switzerland into Italy, where she visited the peaceful Italian lakes. She ate little and slept no matter where. She had learned about such deprivations from the biographies of the saints she had read. When she ran out of money, she simply had her parents come and get her. Bold as she was, she had no fear of their wrath. She escaped again at eighteen to Spain, this time on a bicycle, without a word to her parents.

Worn out, her mother finally decided to send her to work in a fabric shop. Though bored at work, Nini used her time at home to delve into philosophy and to practice piano. She also took a singing class at the Brussels Conservatory and managed to win first prize in a competition. Her basic life principle: never stay still. Keep moving and doing. It was at this uncertain time that Nini gave up the idea of becoming a doctor, listening, for once, to her mother. *"You want to be a doctor? But men themselves know nothing about it, thus, just think, a woman!"* Nini was about to decide to become a nurse, when she met a friend of her father's, an impressive man who initiated her into the history of religions as well as the study of far-away societies (ethnography). That man was Elisée Reclus, a famous geographer and anarchist. He proved to be not only a good person, but also a true mentor. He thus came as a revelation to Nini. Finally defeated, her parents accepted that she would return to England to study. As for Alexandra, she finally was free to live her own life. While it was in London that the East began to take shape, it was in Paris at the Guimet Museum that her vocation finally *"was born."*

At twenty-one, Nini was on her way.

A cup of tea for the Awakened Buddha

According to legend, the tea that drives sleep away came into existence thanks to the Buddha. Each time that he sat down to meditate, reflect upon the world and increase in wisdom, the Buddha would fall asleep. Enormously vexed by this, one day he decided to cut off his eyelids so that he would cease to sink into sleep. His eyelids fell to earth where they sent out roots, which soon sprouted into shoots. As the story goes, it is from the leaves of this plant that tea derives. By her own account, Alexandra was a fervent drinker of the stuff.

CLAUDE DEBUSSY

I was born in 1862 in the classy Parisian suburb of St. Germain-en-Laye to parents with classy names: Manuel-Achille and Victorine-Joséphine-Sophie. But enough joking around. My parents, in fact, were poor and at home there was little to be happy about. When I was three, we moved to Paris, but that didn't make life any easier.

Life was further complicated by the fact that my parents had lots of children (I was the first) even though they could barely put food on the table. Moreover, my father, a courageous but impractical fellow, participated in the Paris Commune on the side of the revolutionaries and ended up in prison for a year. Outside of that stint, he worked as a shopkeeper, printer's assistant, clerk and civil servant.

As for my mother (a seamstress), she soon realized that she couldn't watch over all of her children. Sadly, she found us "*an irritating burden.*" She therefore entrusted two of us to my Aunt Clémentine. Although I got to stay at home with my mother and didn't go to Conservatory until I was ten, the truth is that my mother was very severe, so school might have come as a relief. To crown it all, I was born with a boney tumor on my forehead that formed a large, protruding bump. It wasn't serious, but I was teased about it throughout my early life and called, "the hydrocephalic Christ." For this reason, I always had bangs, and long ones at that. To complete the picture, my father wanted me to be a sailor. It is for all of these reasons that I never was properly educated and have made grammar and spelling mistakes all my life.

When I was eight, my father, who was in prison, met a fellow inmate whose mother, Madame Mauté de Fleurville, claimed to have studied piano with Chopin. As my Aunt Clémentine first had the idea that I should study piano,

CLAUDE DEBUSSY
(1862-1918), French pianist and composer, put his mark on the twentieth century by liberating music from conventional forms. His works, marked by unusual orchestrations, harmonic innovations, fresh tonal perspectives and new rhythms, include such well-known compositions as Prelude to the Afternoon of A Faun, and La mer.

Debussy became famous with his opera *Pelléas and Mélisande,* a project that haunted him for ten years and created quite a scandal. The year: 1902. It wasn't the subject of his opera (the story of un-happy love) that offended the crit-ics and the public. The shock rather came from its musical innovation. As Debussy related it, *"I was accused of having forgotten to leave room in my opera for melody. But in fact, Pelléas is nothing but melody. Only that melody isn't cut and divided into pieces accord-ing to the ancient— and absurd— rules of opera. My melody is intention-ally uninterrupted without any let up because its task is to reproduce life itself. I know very well that not one phrase of my opera can be hummed or whistled. There is no song in life. There are rhythms, atmospheres, and colors, but these, while ceaselessly varying, succeed each other without a break for eternity."*

Debussy with his daughter in Normandy

which I did with a man named Cerutti, it was thanks to her that I was able to continue with Madame Mauté, who thought I had extraordinary musical aptitudes. According to my sister, Adèle, I either played the piano or passed *"entire days sitting in a chair dreaming..."* during a visit to my aunt's in 1871. Even at that young age, music transported me into another reality. In 1872 at the age of ten, thanks to my studies with Madame Mauté, I won a place at the Paris Conservatory. I was one of eight to be chosen out of thirty-nine candidates. After that, I had to agree: I was blessed with extraordinary musical aptitudes.

At Conservatory, it was a different tune. My professor of piano, Monsieur Marmontel, found me *"a charming child, a real artistic talent,"* but I felt he was limited by his tradition bound approach. A year later he continued to find me, *"an excellent sight reader, with a perfectly sure ear, if still somewhat behind on the principles."* In other words, I was quickly con-sidered *"a twelve-year-old prodigy who promised to be a virtuoso of the first order."* To stop there, however, is to fail to see the whole picture, since my relationship with my professor was one of tough love. The old Marmontel was too authoritarian and severe to be a great teacher and for him there was only technique. I, on the other hand, loved to improvise with bizarre chords and unresolved tonalities.

I don't know why, but I felt he wasn't mistaken when he found my manner of attacking the arpeggios rash and unmethodical. Perhaps this was a sign that the piano was to be short lived for me, even though I won 2nd prize for interpretation at fourteen. Composition went better. I also studied harmony with a real fool and music theory with a serious sort (I won 1st prize in score reading at eighteen), but what I liked best was spending time with a sharp, impressive young professor named Albert Lavignac. It was in a mood of pure joy that he taught me the sublime mysteries of solfege (you know, do re me fa so la ti do). No, you're not dreaming, I mean it! Solfege is absolutely amazing when studied beginning from Wagner, and that was what we did. Otherwise, a fellow student, a real idiot, described my music as, "*noisy chromatic passages imitating the buses rumbling down the faubourg Poissonniere.*" Another student later recalled, "*Whether it was through natural maladroitness or through shyness, I don't know, but he literally used to charge at the piano and force all of his effects. He seemed to be in a rage with the instrument, rushing up and down it with impulsive gestures and breathing noisily during the difficult bits.*" As is evident, I wasn't exactly beloved.

Nevertheless, the old stalwart of the Conservatory, Marmontel, was always looking out for storms, and when he saw trouble looming, he acted. Aware that my family was poor and that this made it difficult to manage, he arranged for me to spend the summer as a pianist and accompanist to Nadia von Meck, Tchaikovsky's patroness.

I traveled to Russia, Switzerland, Austria and Italy. I learned. I taught.

I returned to Conservatory full of ideas. My music was found to be "*pretty, but theoretically absurd.*" My response: "*There is no theory. You have only to listen. Pleasure is the law.*"

For all of my detractors and my eccentricities, I continued to hear my own music, and thus I became the famous Claude Debussy.

I may have continued to make spelling mistakes, but it's I alone who composed *Prelude to the Afternoon of a Faun, Pelléas and Mélisande,* and *La mer.*

What was it all about? Beauty, that's what.

The Great Wave by the painter Hokusai, chosen by Debussy to illustrate his score for La mer.

"Listen to the lessons of the wind passing..." Debussy chose nature as his religion. "*I do not practice in accordance with the sacred rites. Before the passing sky, in long hours of contemplation of its magnificent and ever-changing beauty, I am seized by an incomparable emotion. The whole expanse of nature is reflected in my own sincere and feeble soul. ...To feel the supreme and moving beauty of the spectacle to which Nature invites her ephemeral guests, that is what I call prayer.*" In La mer, a symphonic poem (1905), the song of the waves is contrasted with the violence of the wind, to which he gives a magic power: "*Don't listen to anyone's advice, but listen to the lessons of the wind passing and telling the history of the world.*"

WALT DISNEY

Mickey: My dad was named Walter Elias and he was born in Chicago in 1901.

Donald: He wasn't your dad, but mine, and his dad, my grandpa, was Canadian. He already had three brothers when he was born, and his mom taught him at home for a while. When he was four years old, his whole family left the big city of Chicago for a farm in the wide-open spaces of Missouri.

Goofy: He wasn't your father, but mine! And he loved animals and feeding them in the barnyard. He gave them odd names, like Porky, Elmer, and Mortimer.

Mickey: What I know better than any of you is that he started to draw when he was very young, and he drew constantly. He even drew when he didn't have any paper by drawing on toilet paper or on the side of the house using tar!

Minnie: What I can tell you about the person who was really my father is that he adored trains and had many miniature ones as an adult.

Pluto: Woof, woof! (Which is to say he was lucky because he didn't have to go to school until he was around eight, so he had time to draw pictures of animals on the farm.)

All true, but let's leave this little quarrel behind. Suffice it to say that Walt was happy enough to finally go to school because he was eager and curious, but also because his hard-working and worried father was severe and at times even harsh. Walt and his siblings were thus forced to be secretive about a lot of what they did and, on occasion, had to stand up to their dad.

When Walt was nine, his father fell seriously ill. He auctioned off his farm and moved his family back to the city, this time to Kansas City. There he became a newspaper dis-

WALT DISNEY (1901-1966), American film producer, director, screenwriter, animator and businessman, who became one of the most significant creative forces of the 20th century. He created Mickey Mouse, Donald Duck, and Goofy, to name just a few, along with dozens of masterpieces of animation, such as Snow White and the Seven Dwarfs, Cinderella, Pinocchio, The 101 Dalmatians, and The Jungle Book.

je hais
les souris

tributor and hired two of his sons, Roy and
Walt, to work for him. He was an exacting taskmaster and the work was hard, but the family was very poor, so the boys worked and didn't complain.

Mickey: They actually had to wake up at 3:30 am every day in order to deliver all of the newspapers by breakfast time. That's pretty tough on a kid.

At age 10, Walt went to school in Kansas City. He wasn't a particularly good student, largely because he was often tired and sometimes even fell asleep in class. He also doodled and drew a lot of the time.

To make an animated picture
it is necessary to use transparent
sheets of celluloid or plastic, usually
called "cels." These are punched
with two holes that allow them to
overlay each other like pages in a
loose-leaf binder. If the idea is to
show a man falling, then the car-
toonist draws the man standing up
on the first cel. A second cel is
placed on top of the first, where
the shape of the person standing is
traced, while the position of his
limbs is somewhat modified in
order to initiate the movement of
his fall. Thus it goes. Each drawing
is a small step leading to the next.
In an animated cartoon, falling
down takes some time: for a fall of
5 seconds on the screen 120 cels
are required! Today, digitalization
makes it unnecessary to draw most
of those cels. All one needs to do is
to draw the first and the last
frames of the sequence, since the
computer calculates and draws all
of the intermediary steps.

Minnie: In fact, when the teacher asked him to draw flowers, he already gave them faces and arms!

At school, Walt discovered that he loved to dress-up and
perform. He also made a new friend, Walt Pfeiffer.
Together they pursued their interest in theater by perform-
ing skits and participating in amateur shows.
Donald (laughing): They called themselves, "The Two
Walts"!
Goofy: His dad wasn't pleased, and he had to sneak out at
night to perform. His dad didn't think art and theater
were particularly good for a boy, especially not a poor boy
who had to earn a living.
Pluto: Woof! Woof! (Which is to say that his mom always
encouraged him, and he did succeed in persuading his
father to let him enroll in an evening art class.)
Minnie: And don't forget that he also discovered movies
when he was just about fifteen. In 1916, he saw a silent
film called *White Snow*, so naturally he had to make *Snow
White* when he grew up.

Early in 1917, the Disneys prepared to move again, this
time back to Chicago, where Walt's dad was interested in
taking on the operation of a jelly factory. Walt, however,
stayed in Kansas City with his mother and sister to finish
school. He then took a summer job on the railroad as a
"candy butcher," selling newspapers, soda and candy to the
passengers. Despite the long hours of work, he always
found time to draw.
Mickey: His drawings even made it into his high school's
newspaper, *The Voice*, as well as onto the walls of the local
barbershop in Kansas City.
Having joined his family in Chicago, he went to McKinley
High School and took evening classes at The Chicago

Institute of Fine Arts. But the First World War was being fought, and Walt was eager to serve his country. The fact that he was too young didn't stop him. He simply changed his age on his passport and enlisted in the American Red Cross as an ambulance driver.

Minnie: He made it to France! He got there after the Armistice, but there still was a lot to do.

Donald: He was a driver and his ambulance was soon covered from one end to the other with cartoons. He also painted his jacket and soon had a prosperous business drawing on all sorts of things for other people.

Mickey: He also painted German helmets and sold them as souvenirs.

Walt returned to the U.S. at the age of eighteen and joined his family in Chicago. Although he already knew that he had to be an artist, his father wouldn't hear of it. This time, however, Walt stood up to his dad and went to join his brother, Roy, in Kansas City, where he tried his hand at drawing for newspapers. Eventually he got a job with an advertising company. There he met Ubbe Iwerks, another talented artist. Laid off after the Christmas season, they decided to start their own business, which didn't go well. When that folded, they worked together again at the Kansas City Film Ad Company, creating animated advertisements for local movie theaters. Walt also began to make his own animations.

Things were rocky for a while (the Great Depression, endless money problems, and the labor-intensive quality of hand-drawn cartoons), but by the age of twenty-two, Disney was on the train to Hollywood.

A short time later, Mickey Mouse was born, and the rest, of course, is history. Or not quite. Just look around.

Walt is the father of Mickey, Pluto, Donald and the many others who made their first appearance in his black-and-white short films. In 1937, he created the first-ever, full-length animated film in color. It was *Snow White and the Seven Dwarfs*. To do this, 750 artists drew a million frames of characters and scenes over a period of three years. The cost was astronomical, but this risky venture was transformed over night into a fairy tale. Millions of spectators were smitten with the work of the small, artistic Disney studio—the very first animation studio on the planet. Today this empire offers films, theme parks, and toys to children throughout the world.

ALEXANDRE DUMAS

Agreed. I have lived an unbridled, passionate, adventurous, romantic life. The parties, the women, the revolutions! It's true that I also have had time to write dozens and dozens of novels. Even if at times I had assistance, I'm still the author of *The Three Musketeers* and *The Count of Monte Cristo*. Well? Isn't that grand? Still, before getting there, things weren't all that easy. Life can be a real serial, with one drama after another; or, as you might say, a soap. My story begins, I think, with the fact that I was mixed race—neither black, nor white. My father, a military man, came from The Antilles, and my mother from the north of France. A "café au lait," as my type was called in 1802, the year I was born, couldn't just live an easy, peaceful life.

In fact, my delivery itself was difficult, a sign perhaps of things to come. I came out completely blue, which is why I was nicknamed, "Berlick," the name of the devil in a theater piece of the time. Fortunately, things turned around quickly. I adored my father, a real Hercules, and my dog, Truffle. I was too little to understand that my father had been thrown out of the army and that he was sick, very sick. So that he could consult with doctors, we often went to Paris. I was four when my father died from cancer of the stomach. That he was gone made no sense. Nevertheless, when my cousin Eleanor told me that he had departed for the Heavens, I rushed home, seized the paternal pistol and ascended to the attic, shouting: "I'm going to the Heavens! There I will kill the good God who has killed Papa!"

Naturally enough, the serial didn't end there. My family fell into poverty, and because I couldn't go to school, it

ALEXANDRE DUMAS (1802-1870) signed his name to hundreds of works. A past master of the art of historical, adventure fiction, he remains one of the French authors most read throughout the world. At least two of his books (you know which) are now seen as foundational works of popular culture.

The Three Musketeers
made its first appearance as a
newspaper serial in 1844. Each
day, readers were held in suspense
by this story of adventure: the king
asked the queen to wear a jewel to
the next ball that she had already
given to her lover, who had returned
to England. The Musketeers had
only a short amount of time to go
all the way there to try and get it
back. Conspiracies and war did not
help their mission, but offered new
developments for the greatest
reading pleasure. Since most French
people knew how to read as the
result of an 1833 law that opened a
school in each parish, newspaper
publishers competed against each
other for readers. To win the loyalty
of the reading public, one publisher
had the good idea of having a
chapter of a novel appear in his
newspaper each day. Daily paper
sales took off because of this seri-
alization, and his example was
quickly followed. Dumas and
Balzac were the first writers to
exploit the serial novel.

was mother who helped me to learn how to read. I had
already started to learn on my own with a book by Buffon,
which my cousin Eleanor had given me. I spent a lot of
time reading: *Robinson Crusoe*, which was grand, and many
other books about which you'd have no idea since they've
fallen into obscurity.

After my father, my uncle was the man whom I loved the
most. He adored me, as I did him. Still, I was sad and I
cried often. When my mother asked me why, I told her:
"Dumas cries because Dumas has tears."

Eventually things began to fall apart. Short on money and
with no protection, my mother fell into a depression. I
thus was obliged to manage on my own and to educate
myself as best I could. Mostly, I read fantasy stories,
ignoring real literature for the moment. How I loved to
read! I also devoured my mother's stories about my father
the general. As for activities, since my mother had the idea
that I should become a violinist, I went to a music teacher.
After three years I still couldn't get along with the instrument, so my lessons came to an end. Music just wasn't for
me.

At the age of nine, thanks to my mixed heritage, my
mother and the family decided to send me to a religious
boarding school in Soissons. *"What was involved was going
to seminary, which wasn't a simple matter. I couldn't hear reason
when it came to priests."*

I resisted for three months, but finally was defeated and
had to give in. On the day of my departure, I went to buy
an inkpot from a shop where I met Eleanor, who explained
that when I left seminary I would be a priest and that
girls would thus be a thing of the past. What was I to do?
Hmm? Instead of the inkpot, I bought sausage and bread and

went poaching in the forest for three days with one of my buddies, the Old Boudoux.

When I returned, my mother immediately enrolled me in a school in Villers-Cotterêts, the town where I lived. To welcome me, the students dumped a bucket of piss over my head. Suddenly I spent all of my time fighting—because I was mixed race and at age twelve, I still didn't know how to write properly. I remained at school for only two years, which was all to the good, since *"overall, I was not well liked by the other children. I was vain, insolent, arrogant, self-confident, and full of admiration for my little person...."*

The director of my school, an Abbott named Gregory, was both a good and great man who had fought against slavery. He came to our home after my departure from school to teach me Latin. Another master tried to teach me mathematics, which was a disaster, but he praised my handwriting. I liked that, but my mother didn't: *"Writing, writing! ...Every idiot can write well!"* That's exactly what she said. To me! When I think about it...

I was thirteen. In France everything was up for grabs because Napoleon, who had been beaten by the kings of Europe, clung to his throne. I didn't know what to do and was still somewhat uncultivated. Clearly the serial of my life, with its ups and downs, would continue for a while. But I had a secret: I had confidence in myself and somehow that was enough. With the added bonus, perhaps, of my elegant penmanship, which helped me to secure my first real job with the Duc d'Orléans.

"All for one, one for all": the ghosts of Dumas. Already a successful playwright, Dumas understood that to attract a well-known writer, newspaper publishers would pay a lot, even per line. In order not to lose an assignment, it was necessary to work quickly, so Dumas hired a team of writers. He was not the only one to take on such help; however, it was with Dumas that the writers who work in obscurity on novels signed by others came to be called "ghostwriters."

"History is a nail on which I hang my novels," Dumas declared one day. His ghostwriters carried out his historic research for him. They also laid groundwork and conceived of plots. Then the novelist wrote, most often alone, but not always. *The Three Musketeers, Twenty Years After* and *The Vicomte de Bragelonne* were all collaborations, which Dumas finally acknowledged in court.

The Three Musketeers and d'Artagnan

HENRY DUNANT

**The Battlefield at Solferino:
a decisive vision.**
The battles took place in northern
Italy on June 24, 1859. Under
Napoleon III, France fought on the
side of Piedmont-Sardinia against
Austria, which had occupied much
of what is present-day Italy. The
aim was to liberate the Italians
from the Austrians in order to create an independent state. Dunant
had decided to go to Napoleon III's
encampment in Solferino in order
to gain assistance with his business affairs in Algeria. However,
when he arrived in Solferino on the
day after the battle, he forgot the
purpose of his trip. The confronta-
tion had lasted fifteen hours, leaving 40,000 in poor condition and
the wounded on the field where
they had fallen, abandoned by
their generals. To bring them aid,
Dunant created a hospital from
less than nothing, while a friend,
alerted by courier, launched a
contribution drive in the Geneva
newspapers to raise money.
Dunant also interceded with the
emperor so that Austrian doctors
would be free to care for their
wounded.

Henry Dunant was a typical Swiss man who became great. Born in Geneva in 1828 into a rich, honorable, and influential family, Henry was lucky in birth. His father, a merchant, was an important person in the city. A staunch Calvinist, he was involved with orphans and parolees. His wife occupied herself with the sick and the poor.

In so far as he was of a good family, Henry spent a happy childhood with his brothers, sisters, nanny and all the rest of it in a beautiful home. Papa Jean-Jacques was often away attending to business, but happily Mama Antoinette was often around. Her children adored her, even though she read them horror stories about such things as martyrs devoured by lions, as well as the *Fables of La Fontaine*. When she recited *The Wolf and the Lamb*, the young Henry wept profusely. Evidently, he had empathy for victims and the weak even as a child.

Although the Dunants traveled a lot, they never stayed anywhere for long since their trips were largely philanthropic and instructive. As an active and benevolent Christian, Papa Dunant always helped his neighbor. When visiting Toulon, he took Henry to visit and console prison inmates who suffered in terrible conditions. Little Henry was traumatized. At home, orphans came regularly to visit with the family. Of course, the Dunants also gave money to the poor.

In contrast, at the Calvinist school that Henry attended, nobody was particularly charitable towards him. To put it bluntly, he wasn't simply a poor student, but one who had to be held back. Often bored, he sat and dreamed in the warmth of the radiator. In class, he was always the last, in danger of veering off at any moment.

HENRY DUNANT (1828-1910),
Swiss businessman and social activist, who
created the Red Cross. He also helped to
initiate the Geneva Convention on the
wounded and prisoners of war. In 1901
he received the Nobel Peace Prize,
conferred for the first time.

Marked by Solferino, Dunant founded the International Committee of the Red Cross (ICRC), which is at the origin of the "principle of neutrality" of care services and voluntary doctors in times of war. Dunant traveled and promoted his ideas throughout Europe so tirelessly that by 1863 he had succeeded in uniting fourteen countries in an international conference. By that time, however, the president of the Geneva Society for Public Welfare had largely displaced Dunant as the initiative's head, allowing Dunant to function only on the periphery of the event. In the course of that meeting, it was decided that a Red Cross committee would be established in each of the represented countries. It also was decided that all voluntary medical aids would be given a distinctive badge—a white armband with a red cross.

"But, pleaded the child, I have carried off the prize for pity many times! That's not enough explained the school's director. Even to become a pastor, Latin, Greek and Hebrew are necessary." The result: Henry left school definitively at fourteen, without qualifications or a degree and without knowing what he wanted to do later. Within his family, he was called "the banker" because he was somewhat stingy, but that didn't put him on a path either.

While waiting to discover his vocation, he devoted himself to religion. He saw God everywhere, even in the beautiful snowy summits of the Alps that he visited with his friends. He went so far as to organize prayer gatherings at home, but he soon realized that he preferred to help the poor. Therefore, even though he lacked confidence in himself, Henry worked long and hard to found the Christian Union of Young People, an association that quickly took on importance. Around this time, he met Harriet Beecher-Stowe (the author of *Uncle Tom's Cabin*), and threw himself into the fight for the abolition of slavery in the U.S. as well.

Despite all of this activity, Henry's father wanted him to get a job, and he did. Where? Take a guess. Yes, in a bank as an apprentice.

In 1853, Henry was sent on assignment to Algeria, then under French rule. When he returned to Geneva after successfully completing his assignment, he wrote his first book. In 1856, he returned to Algeria, full of grand ideas. Having been granted a land concession, he planned to develop it with the help of foreign investment. His rights, however, were unclear and the colonial authorities weren't interested in helping. Before disaster struck, luck smiled on him through his friendship with Napoleon III's chief of staff, on account of which Dunant decided to meet with Napoleon personally to ask for his help. Faced with this extravagant impulse, so far from protestant rigor and the seriousness of Swiss banking, we might well ponder Henry's chutzpah. Or was it sheer desperation?

Whatever the case might be, he arrived in Italy right after the Battle of Solferino.

His shock was total!

"There were whole battalions of which none were left alive and troops that had been stripped bare of everything; otherwise, water was lacking and their thirst was so intense that the officers and soldiers kept running back to the muddy, dirty horses, covered with dried blood...."

The horror hit Henry with the force of revelation. From that terrible and intense moment on, Henry devoted his life to a campaign that would eventually result in the Geneva Conventions and the establishment of the International Red Cross. Though his initiative was taken over by powerful Swiss politicians and he was robbed of recognition for many years, the dream of persuading countries at war to provide care to the victims scattered across battlefields was his very own. Thus we can say that a single pragmatic, benevolent Swiss man succeeded in saving millions of lives.

The Geneva Conventions. The convention of 1864 was the first of a series of 4 accords, which, taken together, continue to define the rules nations need to respect in regard to wounded, sick or shipwrecked troops and prisoners of war. Twelve countries adopted the Convention of 1864 about the care of wounded and sick soldiers. This accord obliged warring countries to protect and care for all wounded whatever their nationality and provided a legal base for these actions that was recognized by the great European powers. Despite his successes, Dunant was removed from the CICR on account of mishandled business ventures. He lived a solitary life for nearly twenty years before his achievements were definitively recognized. As of 2008, the four conventions have been acceded to by 194 countries and are universally accepted.

THOMAS EDISON

I, Ladies and Gents, was the king of tinkers, a real do-it-yourself enthusiast. I invented plenty of the little things you use everyday with nothing other than my head, my hands and my tools, which I also fiddled around with and improved. I did this all by myself, with almost no schooling. Incredible? No, simple. When you want to do something badly enough you can do it. That's all. Something to consider.

My name is Thomas Alva Edison, and I was born in Ohio in 1847. My family was neither poor nor rich, neither big nor small. I should have been one of seven brothers and sisters but only four survived. Given that decline, perhaps I should have tinkered around in medicine. But okay. No regrets.

When I was seven, we went north to live in Port Huron, which was right near a new railway line. I loved trains not only as a kid, but also as an adult. One can read, sleep, dream and work on trains. It's even possible to set up a laboratory and printing press in a boxcar, as I did. That way I was able to go anywhere. Almost.

Before that, however, I went to school, but only from the age of eight-and-a-half to almost nine. In other words, I went for several months. One day, I returned home in tears because one of my teachers called me addled. Addled! Me! "*I saw then what it is to have a mother. She brought me back to school and announced to the teacher that he didn't know what he was talking about. No boy had ever had a more enthusiastic advocate and all at once I decided to display my dignity to prove that her confidence in me had been well placed.*"

Having taken me out of school, my mother taught me at home. I learned "*...how to read good books quickly and correctly.*" Thus I spent a lot of time reading through my father's library. That was how at age nine, I stumbled across Newton's *Principles*—you know, the famous Newton, who

Let there be light or, the electric light bulb.

Like most inventions, the electric light bulb was not born of a single effort. Before it could come into existence, many other discoveries were necessary. When Edison conceived of his filament bulb, he already knew that a metal wire with a current running through it would warm to the point of giving off light. With this understanding, in 1878 he enclosed a platinum wire within a vacuum (glass globe) and bent it into the shape of a "U." All that remained was to put this platinum wire in contact with wires conducting electricity. Although this gave a good result, there were various problems involved in the use of platinum. By 1879, however, Edison was able to produce commercial bulbs using carbonized bamboo as filament. These bulbs, made possible by the vacuum strength of his glass globes, were able to burn for over 1,200 hours. These electric light bulbs were received with astonishment by a world that had been lit by oil lamp, gas and candles.

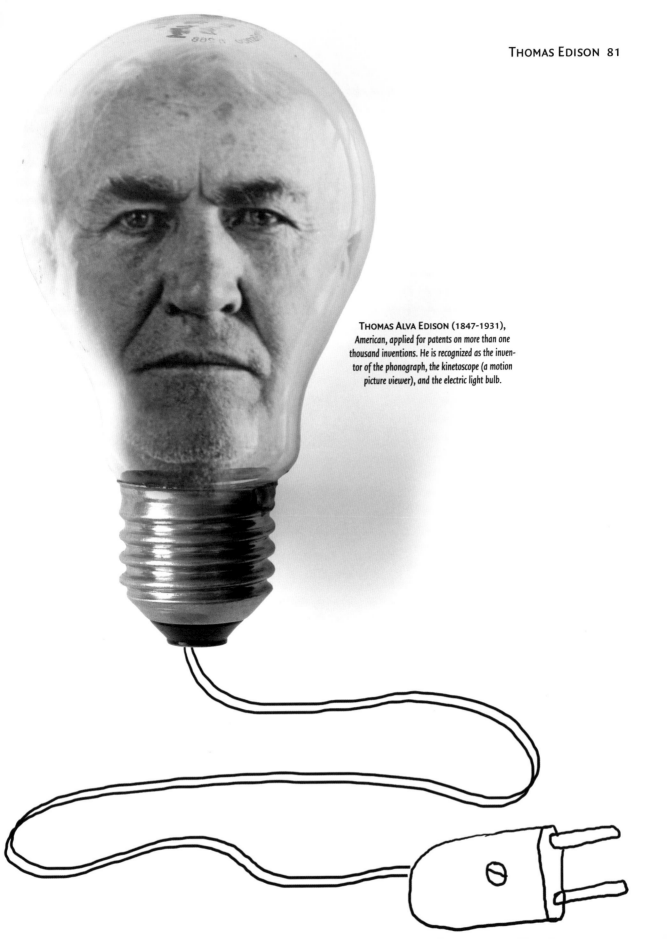

THOMAS ALVA EDISON (1847-1931), American, applied for patents on more than one thousand inventions. He is recognized as the inventor of the phonograph, the kinetoscope (a motion picture viewer), and the electric light bulb.

discovered the laws of gravity when an apple fell on his head. Well, his principles didn't impress me. I concluded, "*if Newton had been less given to abstractions, he would have been able to communicate his knowledge to a far wider audience. This encounter took away my taste for mathematics for good.*"

What fascinated me were mechanical things and chemical concoctions. I built my first laboratory in the basement of our house, where I did all sorts of experiments, many of which failed. Despite several explosions, I was left alone because I was already considered really clever.

I didn't stay put, however, and at age twelve, I got a job as a "candy butcher," selling sweets, magazines and newspapers on the train running between Port Huron and Detroit. As business was good, I recruited my friends to sell veggies and magazines in Port Huron. One day an employee grabbed me by the ears to keep me from falling off the train. I heard something go "pop" inside and that was the last thing I heard, for I was deaf thereafter. Just joking. It's true that I went deaf at twelve, but most likely as a result of the scarlet fever I had as a child.

To continue with my experiments, I installed a laboratory in a corner of the baggage car, where I also printed the newspaper that I wrote and sold. Once the railroad company got wind of this, I had to shut it down, which was hard. All the same, I continued to sell newspapers, which went better and better, particularly because of the Civil War.

One day, in 1862, I had an idea—one of genius, if I do say so myself. It was inspired by my realization that my newspapers sold fastest when big news was breaking. When we came into the station, the Detroit stationmaster gave me important news that he had just received over the telegraph about one of the big battles of the Civil War. I quickly

1877: The Invention of the Phonograph...on Two Sides of the Atlantic The father of the ancestor of the CD player and the iPod is...for the French, Charles Cros, their compatriot, who described the principle of the phonograph before Edison. For Americans, it is Edison, who did in fact complete the first record player. Edison's phonograph worked in this way: a needle passed over the indentations that had been made on a tinfoil-coated cylinder. The sound emitted by the needle as it "read" the indentations was amplified by an acoustic horn. A recording on one of these cylinders lasted for at most a minute.

understood that if the news were wired ahead of me on my return trip to Port Huron that people would rush out to buy my papers when the train came in. I got a large consignment of papers from the editor of the *Detroit Free Press*. The crowds were so large and demand so high that I raised the price of the paper at every station along the way. I made a killing. Swept away by the power of the news wire, I started to learn telegraphy. Before long, I was an itinerant telegrapher, as we were called. I became an expert receiver and quickly advanced to the top of my profession. Naturally, I monkeyed around with the equipment at the companies where I worked in order to improve functioning. I always wanted to move more quickly than others.

On a few occasions things didn't go well, most notably when I invented the end of a telegraph I hadn't received and was shouted out of a place, but I didn't care. After all, I was deaf. In any case, I was so good and so quick that Western Union in Boston hired me. What class! In secret, I continued to tinker around in all directions. As you know, it's important to stay in shape.

I was twenty-one when I made my first great invention: an electric voting machine. It functioned perfectly, but the politicians didn't like it. It went so fast that they would no longer have time to rest. From this I understood that one should only invent useful things that people will buy.

All right, Ladies and Gents, I'll stop here because after that, things really took off. A random list: the light bulb, the electric power system, the cylinder and disc phonographs, telegraph transmitters, projectors, movies—in all, over one thousand things invented or vastly improved by me. Yes, by me. It's true. You can applaud.

The early 1890s: The Invention of Cinema...on Two Sides of the Atlantic
For Americans, Edison is the inventor of movies since it was he who, in 1891, invented the Kinetoscope, the grandfather of the movie camera and the camcorder. By leaning over a Kinetoscope, it was possible to watch a loop of animated images, moved around by the cogwheels inside. For the French, the Lumière brothers are the real inventors of cinema since they were the ones who perfected Edison's machine by creating the "cinematograph," which was much more of a camera and projector. Additionally, they were the first to organize, in 1895, a projection of moving photographic images for the public.

ALBERT EINSTEIN

E=MC²: This formula established the equivalence between mass and energy.
Put otherwise, E and M are two expressions of the same thing, and each can be turned into the other. E = the maximum energy that can be extracted from a body with a mass m (measured in grams, for example) when it is destroyed. C = the speed of light (186,000 miles/second) and ² designates that the square of the speed of light would be 186,000 miles/second X 186,000 miles/second. Since this equivalence becomes clear as things near the speed of light, Einstein chose this speed as his conversion factor. Easy, right?

You know the one with that wild, classic-genius look and lots of unruly hair who sticks out his tongue from the poster tacked up in the lobby? Well, that's Albert Einstein, a genius and one of the greatest physicists of all time. Among other major things, he discovered relativity. Wow! Amazing, right? But wait a minute...it's also because of him that the atom bomb could be made. You're right, but let's talk about other things.

When Albert was born in Ulm, Germany, in 1879, into a bourgeois family, he already had such a large and deformed head that his parents thought he was abnormal. The doctors reassured them, but they remained uneasy, mostly because the big Bebert (also called, Papa Bear) didn't talk before the age of three, or so the story goes. He also seemed to dislike making any effort, and he passed his time building houses out of cards. Life seemed to tire the solitary, dreamy Bebert. Nevertheless, he did wake up from time to time. For example, at age five he was completely captivated by a compass that his father gave him. He also didn't resist learning the violin. All the same, it was clear early on that discipline and Albert didn't go together. At the age of seven, as he watched the German army march past, he cried out: *"When I grow up, I don't want to be one of those unfortunates."* His attitude was just the same at school. *"In elementary school, the teachers acted towards me as if they were sergeants, in high school, lieutenants."* Indeed, school was something of a disaster. He was regarded as slow because he reflected for hours before answering a question, and he didn't seem to be able to learn anything by heart. He also was found to be troublesome, because he really couldn't understand what rules

ALBERT EINSTEIN (1879-1955), German-born physicist, who subsequently held Swiss and then American citizenship. Considered the scientific genius of the 20th century, he won the Nobel Prize in 1921. His theories revolutionized science, as well as our understanding of the world in which we live.

and orders were about. Moreover, he had no interest at all in sports, which was what his classmates were into. In looking more closely, however, we can see that this odd duck adored mathematics and Latin because both are logical. And he was good at them. Very good.

Luckily for him, many visitors passed through the family home. Among them, an engineer uncle, whose every word Albert drank up, and Max Talmud, a medical student, with whom he discussed math and science. From the age of nine, all on his own, he plunged into works of biology, physics, and philosophy, which were infinitely more fun than gym class. Two years later, he discovered a god, that of geometry, namely Euclid. What satisfaction! Then he read Kant. Try it. You'll see...

When he was fifteen, his parents moved to Italy, near Milan, in order to start a new business. At first Albert stayed in Germany in order to finish school and prepare for military service like all the boys his age. A real nightmare.

School continued to seem a very odd thing to Albert. Moreover, as a Jew in Germany, his life as a student had additional strains, for anti-Semitism was around long before Hitler. Consequently, Albert became discouraged. When one of his professors (a truly visionary one) told him he would never amount to anything and should quit school and forget about college entrance exams, Albert did just that. He left at once for Italy, where he joined his parents for pasta. Whether he was expelled or excused from school remains unclear.

Unhappy that his son had abandoned school, his father tried to convince him to become an engineer. Albert agreed to prepare for the entrance exams to the polytechnic in

Zurich. He prepared and failed, receiving a very low overall score. On the advice of the university's rector, he went to prepare again for the exams at a small, peaceful school in Aarau, where, things went better. He was left alone, but also listened to and encouraged. The next time he took the exam, he landed on his feet.

At seventeen, Albert was accepted into the math and physics section of the polytechnic. There he remained heedless and eccentric, with no patience for authority. While he became more and more rigorous in his work, he also got more fed up and did only what was of interest to him. *"You are intelligent, Einstein, but you have a fault: you don't accept that anyone can make a comment to you."* The result: at the end of his studies, he failed to secure a job, while his colleagues were handed professorships.

The reasons for his troubles were always the same—his individualism, his questioning of authority, and his Jewish background.

Little by little, however, things improved: he obtained Swiss citizenship (so long, Germans!), and he was exempted from Swiss military service on account of his flat feet. He also started to give private lessons, founded the Olympia Academy, where scientific and philosophical discussions took place, and, at twenty-one, he got a job at the patents office in Bern. It was a key post. Suddenly he was a sort of inspector of inventions.

The chain reaction had begun.

Mushroom cloud over Nagasaki

It was Einstein's formula E=MC^2 that allowed the Americans to invent the atomic bomb. Nevertheless, the Americans remained suspicious of him, the uncontrollable Jewish pacifist who had fled Hitler's regime in 1933. The first atomic bomb was dropped over the Japanese city of Hiroshima on August 6, 1945. A second was released over Nagasaki on August 9th. These accelerated the end of the Second World War, but opened a new era of nuclear escalation and fear. Einstein protested actively for peace. At the end of his life, he declared, *"If I had my life to live over again, I'd be a plumber."*

GUSTAVE FLAUBERT

"Madame Bovary is I!" Thus Flaubert exclaimed one day. An exaggeration to be sure, since Madame Bovary was the heroine of his novel by that name, and he was a fact that came into the world in Rouen in 1821. "I was born in a hospital [his father, Achille-Cléophas, was its director and chief surgeon] and I grew up in the midst of all human miseries—from which a wall separated us. This perhaps explains why I have ways that are both morose and cynical. I do not love life in the least, and I have no fear of death." Life in a hospital pavilion certainly wouldn't have been cheerful. "The dissecting room of the hospital gave on our garden. How many times my sister and I used to climb the trellis, cling to the vines and peer curiously at the cadavers on their slabs! The sun shone on them, and the same flies that were flitting about us and about the flowers would light on them and come buzzing back to us...."

As if that were't enough, his uncle saw fit to take him to an insane asylum. "Sitting in cells, chained around the middle, naked to the waist, disheveled, a dozen women were screaming and tearing their faces with their nails. I was then perhaps six or seven." An upsetting sight for a young boy.

How did Flaubert write about his childhood later on? By describing himself as cheerful, given to laughter, and in love with his mother, horses, carriages, and drums.

Gustave admired his father, who was kindly, but most interested in his eldest son, a big shot and a brilliant student. Fortunately for Gustave, who was passive, fragile and highly imaginative, his nanny, Julie, was there to spoil him. (Later, Flaubert used her as a model, most notably for Felicity in his story, *A Simple Heart*). Gustave passed his days listening to Julie's stories, bits about history, love and ghosts. He also spent time at the neighbors, where the grandpapa read him *Don Quixote*. This made it harder for him to learn how to read than it was for his little

GUSTAVE FLAUBERT (1821-1880), remains one of the greatest French writers of all time. He is credited with "inaugurating the modern novel." When his book, **Madame Bovary**, appeared in 1857, he had to stand trial..

Madame Bovary creates a scandal!
Flaubert's heroine, Emma Bovary, feasts upon novels during her youth, taking them literally. A disappointed wife and the mother of a family that has failed to knit together, she desires a more exalted life. This dream catapults her into passionate but fatal love affairs. Once ruined, she poisons herself with arsenic. When the novel appeared in 1857, it was attacked as "*an offence against society and religious morality and an affront to decent comportment.*" Its heroine was judged immoral, as was its author for having depicted her adventures so directly. Flaubert was put on trial, but acquitted with a reprimand, and the publication of his book went forward. It became, of course, a best seller. The trial gave him great publicity, but for the wrong reasons. Neither the power of his writing, nor his extraordinary description of the human capacity for self-delusion lay behind the book's popular success. (You can guess why sales were so high.) Flaubert, hardly an opportunist, remained hurt by the events.

A caricature of Flaubert dissecting Emma Bovary

sister. "*How will you learn if Papa Mignot reads?*"

When Gustave was eight, he made his first great friend, Ernest Chevalier, with whom he frequently corresponded. At ten, he began to write plays—tragedies (look at that), which he performed for his family, assisted by Ernest and his sister, Caroline. He also composed historical and philosophical works.

At the local school, however, where Gustave boarded at age eleven, life was hard. Finding the rules overly severe, he showed himself to be wild and undisciplined. Often at the bottom of his class, he excelled only in history, where he was at the top. Socially, his classmates excluded him, and his teachers pestered and punished him. Perhaps the one benefit of being a boarder was that he had a lot of time to read, a huge amount really.

Slowly things improved, with a good grade in Latin here, an honorable mention in geography there. Gustave's scorn of grammar led things to get out of hand with his French professor, Dugazon, but as he was a kindly man he helped Gustave make progress. In time, Dugazon even became something of a mentor.

On vacation in Trouville, the fifteen-year-old Gustave fell madly in love with Elisa Schlesinger, who was twenty-six. His passion not only consumed him over the course of the relationship, but also marked him for life. Later he wrote about it in his novel, *Sentimental Education*. Rather than paralyzing him, this dose of mad love inspired him. Under its influence, he wrote more and even published short pieces in the local paper, *Le Colibri*. He devoured books with great appetite, above all Rabelais and Byron "*the only two who have written in a spirit of malice toward the human race and with the intention of laughing in its face.*"

Equally passionate about the theater, Gustave blackened heaps of pages with ink.

Finally at seventeen, he no longer had to board at school. All that remained was for him to take the baccalauréat exam and go to law school, as his father had decided he would. Repulsed by the idea of becoming a lawyer, he wrote to his friend Chevalier, who was already at college in Paris: "*What do you expect to become? What will your future be? Do you ask yourself that, sometimes? No: why should you? And you are right. The future is the worst thing about the present. The question, 'What are you going to do?', when it is cast in your face, is like an abyss in front of you that keeps moving ahead with each step you take. Quite apart from the metaphysical future (which I don't give a damn about...), there is the future of one's life. But don't think that I am undecided as to the choice of a profession: I am quite resolved to embrace none whatever.*" You get the tone.

As it happened, he passed the bar, went traveling, which he loved, and then went to law school. Once there, he immediately began to fall apart, developing epilepsy, which allowed him to drop out and return home.

Moreover, sorrow was on the prowl once again. In 1846, within a few months, Gustave lost his father, (after which his epileptic fits began to abate), his sister and his best friend, Alfred (first through marriage, then death). The Grim Reaper was there once again, as it had been in childhood. Again life appeared to Gustave as no more than "death on the march." What was different was that instead of being done in by this, he was annoyed. Otherwise, while patiently awaiting his ineluctable end, he was driven by one desire: to attain perfection. Not in life, but literature.

Read his novels. You be the judge.

Dictionary of Accepted Ideas (extracts)

Flaubert worked on his *Dictionary of Received Ideas*, which includes a *Catalog of Fashionable Ideas*, while writing his novels. His entries reveal his satiric wit and his talent for depicting stupidity.

A

ADOLESCENT – Never begin a scholastic prize-giving speech other than with "Young adolescents" (which is a pleonasm).

ANGEL – Works well in love and literature.

APRICOTS – We won't have any again this year..

B

BACK – A clap on the back can give you tuberculosis.

BEARD – Sign of strength. Too much beard makes one's hair fall out. Useful for protecting neckties.

BOOK– No matter which one, always too long.

C

CAMEL – Has two humps and the dromedary has one. Or else, the camel had one hump and the dromedary has two. It gets confusing.

CHIAROSCURO –We don't know what this is.

CHIVALRY – It's dead.

COMPASS - Having a good internal one helps you walk straight.

OLYMPE DE GOUGES

Ah, how beautiful Olympe was, and she profited from it. She was intelligent and generous, and at the height of the French Revolution, she fought against slavery and took the part of her own sex. She was a woman of heart with a good head, even though Robespierre saw fit to cut the latter off.

Marie Gouze (her real name) was born in Montauban in 1748. Her mother, a washerwoman who married the butcher Pierre Gouze, had a lover named Jean-Jacques Lefranc de Pompignan, a local magistrate. How did Marie account for that later, once she had become Olympe? By accepting the truth: *"What expressions might I use so as not to offend modesty, precedent and the law by revealing the truth? The fact is that my mother, a married woman, gave herself to a man with whom she already had been in love as a girl, whom she adored and wished to marry, except that he was separated from her and sent to Paris, from where he returned celebrated, certainly, but not cured of his passion. That her husband was away at precisely this moment further favored the renewal of their liaison...."*

Just as everyone in town knew that Marie was Pompignan's daughter, Pierre Gouze knew it too. In the provinces, however, people made as few waves as possible, so the matter wasn't discussed beyond the whispers of local gossip. When Gouze died two years later, Pompignan was prohibited from raising his illegitimate daughter, so Olympe's mother married a policeman, whom little Marie didn't like at all.
The result, no father—not real, false, or new. For a little country girl, things were already pretty complicated. Perhaps that's why she came to guard this principle in stone: be suspicious of marriage, *"the tomb of trust and love."*

At the Convent School in Montauban, Marie learned to

The French Revolution...of Men
The people were hungry and over-burdened with taxes, and the nobles no longer wanted an absolute monarch. The bourgeoisie profited from these circumstances by seizing power. This led to the fall of the Ancien Régime, of the king, of the privileges of the nobility and of the clergy. In 1789, the *Declaration of the Rights of Man and of the Citizen* symbolized this rupture. It's first Article affirmed, *"All men are born free and equal in rights,"* but women were to remain the property of their fathers and husbands, without the right to vote, and deprived, of course, of the right to sit in political assembly. Among the great men of the Revolution, only the mathematician Condorcet publicly expressed his indignation at this.

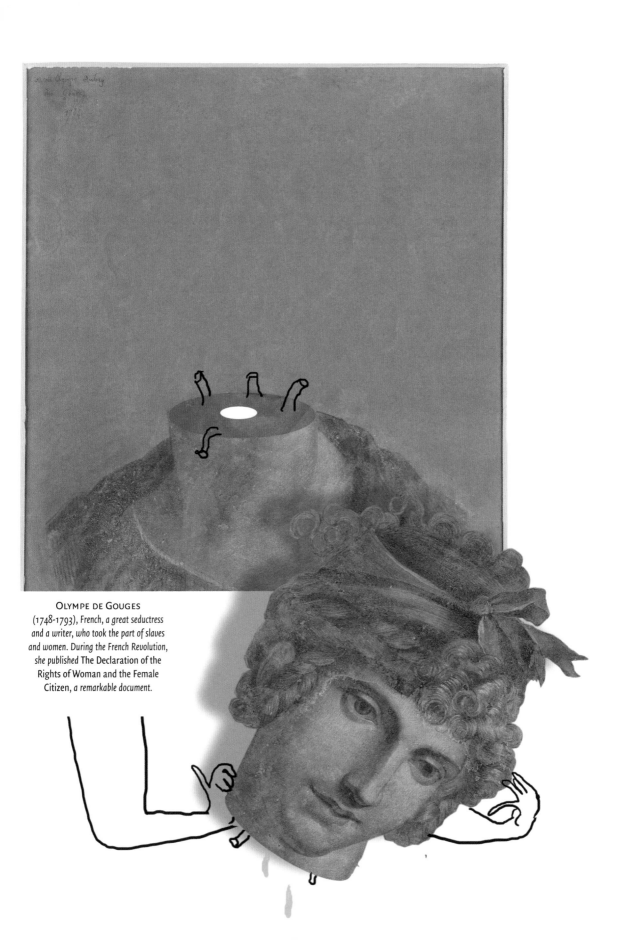

OLYMPE DE GOUGES
(1748-1793), French, a great seductress
and a writer, who took the part of slaves
and women. During the French Revolution,
she published The Declaration of the
Rights of Woman and the Female
Citizen, a remarkable document.

The Declaration of the Rights of Woman and the Female Citizen.
Olympe de Gouges was a moderate. She was, for example, against the killing of the king during the Revolution. Writing was the one weapon available to her for engaging in politics, and within five years, she published sixty-odd articles in the newspapers.

In 1871, all on her own, she wrote, published and distributed her version of the *Declaration*: "Woman is born free and remains equal to man in rights." The *Declaration of the Rights of Woman and the Female Citizen* was read and approved in all of the women's assemblies that had been formed since 1789 in support of the Revolution. Strongly feminist and thus revolutionary in outlook, her *Declaration* called for full equality between the sexes in private and public life. Unfortunately, though predictably, its echo didn't carry far enough.

read and write somewhat. Although she became a devoted reader and a prolific writer, her spelling, grammar, and penmanship remained poor, which is probably why she dictated her works. Other than that, we don't know much about her schooldays outside of her own confessions: "*I was taught nothing, raised in a part of the country where French is poorly spoken, and so I do not understand its principles. I know nothing. Errors of French, of construction, of style, of knowledge, of spirit, of intellect.*" Olympe always came across a bit strong. "*I make a trophy of my ignorance; I dictate with my soul, never my mind. The natural stamp of genius is in my productions.*" A full program.

At sixteen, she was given away in marriage, against her will of course, to the cook of the king's steward. Her husband, whom she found repugnant and didn't love, was neither rich nor well-born. What recommended him? He was a great friend of her brother's. You get the picture. She became pregnant quickly enough, but her husband died shortly thereafter (we don't know how). With his departure, she breathed a great sigh of relief. "*I was eighteen, my husband was dead—peace to his soul. He was an idiot and we didn't love each other at all.*" From Olympe, only the truth, however brutal.

The essential thing: Montauban was finished.

Finally on her own, she changed her name. Olympe de Gouges must have seemed a much classier name for a beautiful, young widow. She took a lover, a rich man from Lyon, named Bietrix de Rozieres, and she went to Paris. At last!

On her own and provided for, she led the good life in Paris. Able to spend lavishly, she lived a full life of social engagements and chaotic love affairs (she was nicknamed "the doe"). She attended salons where she played games and was entertained, as well as literary and political salons where she met artists, philosophers and writers. A woman of energy and spirit, she cultivated herself and developed her mind. She read Rousseau with passion. Her taste for freedom and equality led her to believe in a better world, denounce poverty, and defend the oppressed.

She devoted at least ten years to educating herself, becoming enamored of the philosophers of the Enlightenment in the process. Her lovers didn't really understand her, but they accepted her. They even helped her to publish (an epistolary novel denouncing the idleness of the provincial aristocracy) and to have her work staged (a piece against slavery that created a scandal). She became both well known and widely attacked. She was mocked, for example, for her love of animals, which she looked upon as punished humans. She also was ridiculed for her feminism, but she didn't give a hoot, and she continued to write quickly and a lot.

Then the French Revolution erupted.

Olympe put all of her energy and fortune into writing and publishing articles in defense of women. *"As woman has the right to mount to the scaffold, she ought equally to have the right to mount to the Tribune."* Still she remained a moderate, deeply suspicious of the male radicals (the Montagnards and Jacobins) who organized the Terror. Little by little, she set them against her.

In response, these radicals sent Olympe to the guillotine. Dead but not forgotten, if not exactly acknowledged either, Olympe was way before her time when it came to sisterhood. Brava, or right on!

From Revolution to Terror

After 1789, France lived according to the ups and downs of the struggles between opposing political groups. Olympe remained close to the moderates, who were called the "Girondins." These, however, were quickly eliminated by the "Montagnards," who were always ready to spill blood to defend their idea of the Revolution. Beginning in 1793, the Terror heightened and arrests, trials, and condemnations increased. Despite this climate of extraordinary violence, Olympe continued her activities. She organized gatherings and marches in defense of women and their rights. But the year 1793 was fatal to all who refused to conform to the ideas and actions of Robespierre, the strongman of the moment. Arrested, imprisoned, and found guilty, Olympe de Gouges was executed by the guillotine in 1793.

JOHN LENNON

I am one of the Beatles. No, not Paul. The other one, John. OK?

I was born in Liverpool, England, at the time of the Second World War, during one of the worst German bombing raids, which produced a most dreadful music. In a burst of patriotic enthusiasm, I was given "Winston" as a middle name, in tribute to Churchill who was leading the country. My dad, who was in the Navy, wasn't around for my birth, but I met him a few times before my parents split when I was four.

My mother, Julia, met another man, but things were complicated, so she put me in the care of her sister, Mimi, and her husband, George. They took really good care of me, though Mimi was a little severe.

"My auntie... lived in the suburbs in a semidetached place with a small garden and doctors and lawyers and that ilk living around, not the poor, slummy kind of image that was projected. I was a nice, clean-cut, suburban boy, and in the class system that was about a half a niche higher class than Paul, George, and Ringo, who lived in government-subsidized houses." Compared to them, I was spoiled.

My dad reappeared when I was five and took me away from Mimi with the idea of secreting me away to New Zealand, but Julia tracked us down. Given the choice between him and Julia, I finally chose my mom, who brought me back to Mimi's. Imagine!

At six, I went to school in Allerton, a neighboring suburb. I may have been argumentative and difficult, but I wasn't a bad student. After all, I used the counting songs

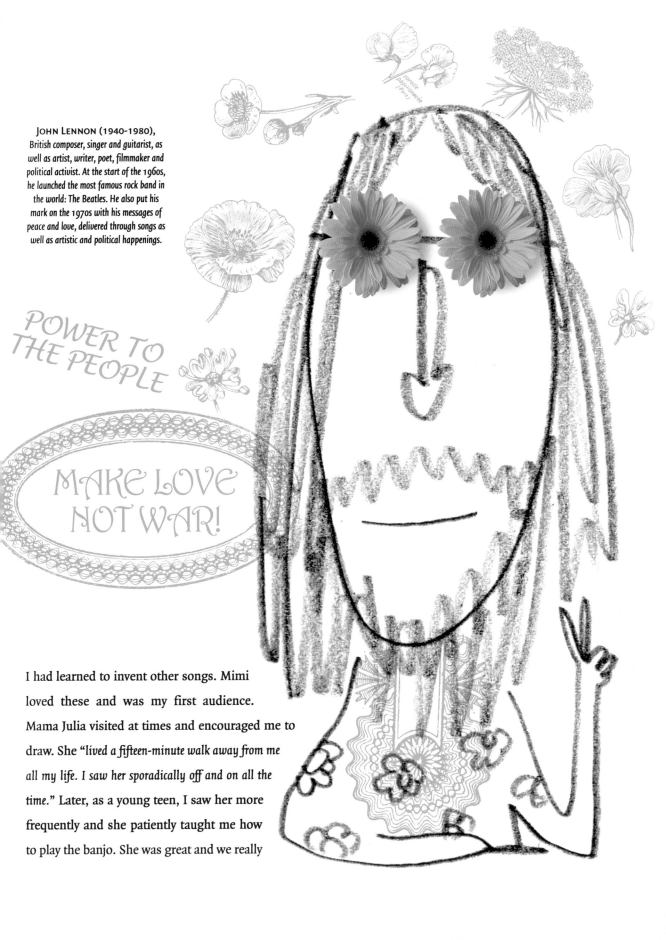

POWER TO
THE PEOPLE

MAKE LOVE
NOT WAR!

I had learned to invent other songs. Mimi
loved these and was my first audience.
Mama Julia visited at times and encouraged me to
draw. She "lived a fifteen-minute walk away from me
all my life. I saw her sporadically off and on all the
time." Later, as a young teen, I saw her more
frequently and she patiently taught me how
to play the banjo. She was great and we really

got on. We shared the same ironic sense of humor. I hung out at her house, where I heard "*Rock Around the Clock*" for the first time. Dancing in the kitchen, she told me, "*This is the kind of music I love!*" Fate? Yeah, perhaps...

At this time, I attended the Quarry Bank Grammar School where I was bored: "*A poor result due to the fact that he spends most of his time devising 'witty' remarks,*" was the comment of one of my teachers. It's true that I preferred drawing to studying and that I was easily distracted and failed all of my exams. I also fought a lot and did some really stupid things. Shame on me! However, if I was a rebel, I also was someone who read a lot. As Mimi put it, "*His mind was going the whole time. It was either drawing, or writing poetry, or reading. He was a great reader. It was always books, books, books....*"

"We are more popular than Jesus Christ," said John Lennon. It was almost the truth: in October 1963 the crowd that came to welcome The Beatles at the London airport disrupted traffic throughout the city. With this, "Beatlemania" was born. Thousands of fans adopted "the look" of the Beatles and provoked riots at their appearances all over the world. Beyond their appearance, the Beatles became a symbol of freedom and independence from the old guard. By turning out for their concerts and buying their records by the millions, young people asserted themselves against an authoritarian and adult society. The four Beatles also made movies and were decorated by the Queen of England. In 1966, Lennon met the artist Yoko Ono, who overturned his life and that of the group by encouraging him to turn the page. The Beatles' last concert took place in San Francisco in August 1966. The Beatles split up in 1970.

John, George, Ringo and Paul: The Beatles

In other words, I was passionate about serious things, which included music. I formed my first group, *The Black Jacks*, at school. After a while, we became *The Quarry Men*, a skiffle group that played American folksongs on electric guitars and improvised. (Later this group came to include Paul McCartney and George Harrison, another really good guitarist.) "*The guitar's all very well, but you'll never make a living out of it,*" Mimi worried. A valid concern, certainly, in response to which, we quickly and justifiably gave ourselves over to rock and roll. "*We all had seen Elvis at the movie theater, surrounded by all those girls, and we said, 'now there's a good job!'*" Yeah, yeah, yeah,

It was when we played a garden party at St. Peter's Church that I first met Paul McCartney. "*You know it was the day when I sang 'Be Bop A Lula' in front of an audience for the first time. After the show, we talked, and I saw he had talent. He was playing the guitar backstage.... I turned right 'round to him on first meeting and said, 'Do you want to join the group?' and I think he said yes the next day."*

As fate would have it, it was around this time, just when I was re-establishing my relationship with my mum (playing the banjo and all that) that she was run over by a car driven by a drunk, off-duty cop. For me, this was a catastrophe that *"absolutely made me very, very bitter."* My entire world turned upside down. I was around sixteen and at Liverpool Art College where nothing much happened with my art. I did, however, keep myself *"well entertained."* I also met my first wife, Cynthia, and found a soul mate in Stuart Sutcliffe, who became a Beatle before love and death in Germany.

One two! One, two, three, four! In 1960, the Indra Club, a nightclub in Hamburg, gave us a contract for 100 pounds sterling a week for each of us. Before leaving, we changed our name from *The Silver Beatles* to *The Beatles*. It was difficult for our families to accept Germany. After all, Hamburg was a city of sin. Once there, we discovered that our repertory was too short, so we sang our own songs. It was delirium! *"I was raised in Liverpool, but grew up in Hamburg,"* where a lot happened. We were thrown out of the Indra for being too loud, we met Ringo Starr, we lost Stuart to a woman and a couple of us got deported. We returned home to England very much changed, but we still were far from suspecting that we'd make it to the *"toppermost of the poppermost"* and that our name would become a global myth.

Rock & Roll will never die! OK?

...and their fans in 1965

Imagine...John, the pacifist
While Paul McCartney wrote incomparable melodies that spread throughout the entire world, Lennon was the "thinking-head," the intellectual of The Beatles. He was the one who persuaded his comrades to renounce the scene and then the group. After The Beatles, he wrote songs that developed innovative rhythms. His lyrics also evolved, transmitting the ideas of Flower Power, the hippie movement. Living in New York with Yoko Ono, Lennon stood against violence, racial segregation, and the Viet Nam War as well as for the emancipation of women. In 1980, an unstable groupie named Mark David Chapman killed Lennon right outside his apartment building. After 9/11 it was reported that his hymn to peace, *Imagine*, still so powerful, had been put on a no-play list by the corporate owner of more that 1,200 radio stations.

ABRAHAM LINCOLN

I will tell you how one becomes the 16th president of America. God Bless You. The one who managed to abolish slavery, even if the result was the Civil War, a real butchery between North and South.

At first it was necessary to be born in 1809 in Kentucky, an area just about in the middle of the country. Kentucky's location is important because it was at the time a "frontier state," which is to say that in neighboring states slavery still existed. At home in our state, it had been abolished. The next condition for becoming the 16th president: poverty, misery and unhappiness. My parents were illiterate, my little brother died very quickly after birth, and the family motto was: work. Not at school, mind you, but in the fields. What was I to start? A young agricultural worker.

When I was around six, or perhaps seven, I learned how to read a little at the Cumberland Road School, where I went with my sister. We didn't go to school for very long, however, as the family emigrated to Indiana, a state just next door to Kentucky. It was a wild region with many wild bears and other animals still in the woods. At night, the bears came to attack our pigs.

We lived in a cabin, so life was worse than before. I spent my time clearing the ground of undergrowth, trimming boards and cutting wood. It was a hard life. "*My father taught me to work, but he never taught me to love it.*" When I was nine, my mother died, which was terrible, of course. My father returned to Kentucky, where he stayed for nine months, leaving my sister and I alone in Indiana. I was twelve, but already a man. When father returned, he brought with him a new wife and mother, Sarah Bush Johnston by name. She had three children and a personality with which to reckon. Curiously, and luckily, she

ABRAHAM LINCOLN (1809-1865), elected president in 1860, he abolished slavery in 1863. As soon as he was elected, fearful of his ideas, the Southern states, which wanted slavery to continue, declared that they would secede from the Union. With this, the Civil War had begun.

The tearing apart of a young nation.

After American independence in 1776, slavery was abolished little by little in the industrial states of the North and the East, but not in the South. There numerous small and medium-sized farmers and a handful of large landowners exploited slaves on their cotton and tobacco plantations. Some Americans protested against this barbarous practice. This led to the Civil War (1861-65), between the pro-slavery forces of the South, which wanted to secede from the Union, and the abolitionists of the North.

became "*the best friend I ever had.*" I continued to work in the fields, even though I liked it less and less. In fact, my spirit flagged to such an extent that my father, who wanted me to become a farmer, began to think of me as a parasite.

What kept me going was the fact that I was curious, very curious. I listened to the conversations of the adults around me and I tried to understand everything they said by asking a million questions. Until the age of fifteen, I went to school only between the winter harvest and the planting for spring, so only very occasionally. All in all, I probably ended up with about a year and a half of formal schooling. I went to a "*blab school,*" so-called because learning was by rote memory and aloud. "*There was absolutely nothing to excite ambition for education. Of course when I came of age I did not know much. Still somehow I could read, write and cipher to the Rule of Three (i.e. solve for a fourth term when three are known): but that was all.*" Not quite all, perhaps, because at school, I also discovered a love of reading. My interest was so keen that I walked miles to borrow a book—an adventure story, like *Robinson Crusoe,* the *Bible, Aesop's Fables,* or a book about George Washington, another American president.

At the home of the sheriff of my town, I also dug up many legal texts, which I devoured, especially the *Declaration of Independence* and the *Constitution of the United States.* "*He who lends me a book is my friend,*" of this I was sure. I also read the dictionary, which I highly recommend. It's a really good book. Moreover, I adored poetry, and even wrote some verse. I swear it.

When I was seventeen, I left home and was hired as a ferryman on the Ohio River. I made a little money, which I sent on to my father. I also found myself before a judge one day, since there are times when one is obliged to not be entirely within the law. From that moment on, little by little, I began to wander among the cabins that served as courts, and I became more and more interested in those who were lawyers by profession. Law , which teaches logical reasoning and clear expression, excited me.

When I was twenty-one, my father moved again, this time to Illinois. I accompanied him. Once there, however, I realized that he still wanted me to become a farmer. For the first time in my life, I told him: no! From that time on, life really began. Not that it was easy. I took many different jobs, undertook many journeys, and was often discouraged. Eventually, however, in the small city of New Salem, I succeeded in becoming Postmaster, following which I was able to break into political life. That happened, I think, because I loved politics and because I spoke well and people were able to understand me. I did not yet know that my road would finish in the presidency.

The day I was elected president, at age 51, I told the journalists, *"Well, boys, your worries have ended; now mine begin."* This proved only too true. First, the war; second, my assassination in 1865 by a Confederate sympathizer. Despite the war and my death, I still won, however, for it was on account of my efforts that the slaves were legally emancipated.

Of course, the realization of their freedom would take a lot more time, and I left many more legal battles to be fought, but I changed the terms. Let's not forget the power of the law.

One in ten inhabitants of the United States was a slave on the eve of the Civil War. Slaves had no rights. The children born of a slave mother became the property of the slave owner, who at times even separated families. Slaves couldn't marry or move without the permission of their master. They also were forbidden to learn how to read and write. Even if the law held out that possibility, it was the rare landowner who gave his slaves this freedom. Even though law prohibited corporal punishment, whipping, mutilation, and even death would go unpunished. We can only imagine the tremendous courage of the slaves who resisted or escaped for the north and the east of the country.

JACK LONDON

In the past, when writers weren't celebrities and didn't yet have the cache to captivate the public, an authentic American writer had to really work. Often poor, they took up all sorts of different jobs in order to make ends meet. Living among workers who were equally poor, they became vaguely socialist. This was called "roughing it."

John Griffith London (let's call him Jack right from the start) was born in San Francisco in 1876. His young life began with quite a punch, giving him ample material to write about, even though he was too young to do so. First off, he didn't know his father; second, his mother tried to commit suicide before he was born; third, he was sent away to a wet nurse. Fortunately his nurse, Mrs. Virginia Prentiss, was kind and gentle, for he was with her when he fell so ill that he lost all of his hair. *"My hair grew back completely white, so entirely so that my wet nurse, who was black, called me Cotton Ball."* Jack was eight months old when a man named John London, a sewing machine salesman with two daughters, married his mother and gave him a home.

Having succeeded in enlarging his family, John London abandoned his business to grow vegetables. As for Jack's mother, who suffered from mood swings and break-downs, she demonstrated little affection for Jack, showing interest only in the spiritualism that concerns itself with tables that turn and spirits that speak through moving glasses. At age four, Jack was happy to go to school because his home was *"the house of phantoms,"* where an Indian chief spirit named Plume often prowled. At school in Oakland, CA, Jack was considered a nervous child.

When he was six, his parents moved to a ranch. For him that meant hard work after school. It was at this time that he met and befriended a fellow named John Barleycorn, who would follow him for a long time. John Barleycorn

JACK LONDON (1876-1916), an American journalist and writer, known mainly for having written White Fang and Call of the Wild, two children's classics. Through his work he denounced the hardships of life in an America that was rising in terms of global power, while facing many inequalities at home. Extraordinarily popular in his own time, he was a larger than life figure.

Gold: During much of the 20th century, the dream of finding gold drew a large number of people out West, especially to California. There, in 1848, the discovery of nuggets in the Sacramento riverbed spurred prospectors from the entire world over to brave great distances and dangers. These prospectors were rarely lucky because the beds were quickly monopolized by large industrial concerns. The Americans, Europeans and Chinese who went to try their luck lived in camps governed by the strongest, most merciless law—the law of the West. These prospectors founded towns and contributed to the development of the state of California. Gold fever spread throughout the country, even to the Klondike, in the frozen wilderness of Alaska, where new beds were found in 1896.

was the playful name that Jack gave first to beer and later to stronger stuff.

After a time, his parents moved once again, this time to raise chickens in Livermore, a backwoods. As luck would have it, Jack liked his new school a great deal and all at once he became interested in books. His appetite was first whet by the Washington Irving novel, *Stories of Alhambra*. "*From age four to nine, I lived on ranches in California. I learned to read and to write around age five, but I don't remember how that happened. It seems to me that I've always known how to read and write and I have no earlier memory. According to my parents, I insisted on being taught. I was an omnivorous reader, mostly because reading matter was rare, and I gratefully accepted all that came into my hands.... I should add that life on a ranch in California was not a great stimulant to the imagination.*" As it turned out, raising chickens was a failure, so the family returned to Oakland. Nevertheless, Jack's daily life didn't change much. He continued to read, write and get into fights. He was a rebel, both opinionated and proud. Poor and poorly dressed, it was with his fists that he won respect. That's how it was. He certainly wasn't going to succeed in proving himself through his book learning.

Nonetheless, he held onto books hungrily. Not only did he become a regular at the local library, known by everyone, but he also became good friends with the librarian, Ina Coolbright. Little by little he exhausted the entire shelf of travel and adventure stories.

It was at this time that his parents moved again. Jack was ten and already had to work. To help support the family, he sold newspapers and gave all of his earnings to his mother. In order to have a dollar, he took other small jobs.

Nevertheless, he hung on at school, even managing to graduate from grammar school.

At age fourteen, he left school to work in a pickle factory. He worked 14-16 hours a day for miserable pay, often getting drunk after work in the local saloons.

From then on, London did just about anything. He worked as an oyster pirate and a fish patroller (chasing poachers); he got into brawls and became a member of a gang (The Road Kids). As a pirate and patroller, he practically lived on San Francisco Bay. Then he spent several months on a sealing schooner. Having survived a terrible typhoon in Japan, he wrote *Story of a Typhoon off the Coast of Japan*, for which he won 1st prize in the San Francisco Best Descriptive Article Contest. He was seventeen. As a gang member, he became a hobo, hopping trains, riding the rails for free and adopting socialist views as a member of the unemployed. Thus things went until he got into a bad brawl and ended up imprisoned for vagrancy.

Taking stock of himself, he decided that education was going to save him. At nineteen, he briefly went to high school, but was kicked out for his involvement in socialist politics. Having educated himself well in libraries, he nevertheless managed to gain admittance to the University of California at Berkeley. He stayed for only six months, leaving either on account of the students (foolish and egotistical) or because he had to work.

Jack already knew that he wanted to write, but he understood that first he had to live. Having been a factory worker, pirate, patroller and vagabond, he proceeded to work as an electrician, laundry worker, groom, and gold prospector.

And he did all of that without ever ceasing to read.

Fever in Alaska

Jack left Berkeley, California, for the Klondike in 1897 after the discovery of gold. To reach veins deep in the earth on your own land is an achievement in itself. To travel 600 miles to reach them, as the twenty-one-year-old Jack did, is another order of hardship entirely. Men went on foot and by boat, carrying weapons, a tent, and provisions to last for many months. On the trip, it was necessary to go quickly as winter was approaching. Once there, the conditions of life were appalling (as in Chaplin's *The Gold Rush*), and Jack fell ill before having found a single nugget of gold. He survived and learned a lot about himself. "*It was in the Klondike that I discovered myself. Nobody spoke. Everybody thought. In such circumstances you see things in their true light. I saw them thus for myself.*" In his story, *To Build a Fire*, London plunges the reader into the treacherous arctic cold and describes the greed that transformed humans into beasts. The Klondike serves as the setting for other stories as well as the novel, *White Fang*

Hard going in the Klondike

PABLO PICASSO

Seeing from Many Perspectives

At the beginning of the twentieth century, Cézanne painted objects from life by recomposing them into geometric forms. As an old man, the painter declared: "*Now I can no longer try to have the young understand my method.*" But Picasso, who knew him, had something quite different to say: "*He is the father of us all.*" But Picasso went even further than Cézanne. For example, when Picasso painted a face, he drew it as he saw it, but on the very same plane he also sketched what he would see if the face were in profile. Fascinated by African masks, Picasso took from them a lesson in stylization, having understood that the originality and personality of a person, an object or a landscape could best be conveyed through the clear rendering of carefully selected traits.

Bull's Head (bicycle seat and handlebars)

His real name is Pablo Diégo José Francisco de Paule Juan Nepomuceno Maria de los Remedios Crispiniano de la Santissima Trinidad Ruiz-Picasso. Fortunately, all we need to remember is Pablo Picasso. He was born in 1881 in the south of Spain, in Malaga, the city of grapes. When he was just a baby, he already was thought to be handsome and women (his mother, his aunts, and his sisters) adored him, even though he didn't yet walk or talk. Rather, he spent a lot of time watching his father draw. Interestingly, his very first word was "lapiz" (pencil), though he only really said "piz" since speech wasn't to be his thing.

The young Pablo adored his father, "Pepe" in Spanish. This elegant, witty man was a professor of drawing and an amateur artist, who became the curator of a museum and a restorer of old canvases. "*My father made paintings for the dining room, the type where you see partridges and pigeons, hares and rabbits and feathers.*" Pablo, an inventive and bossy child, followed his father everywhere, even to the bullfight!

When it came time for Pablo to go to school, it quickly became clear that school was not for him. To deal with that, he was sent to a private school, the most fashionable in the city, but things didn't go well there either. Whereas the other students paid attention in class, he spent all of his time drawing pigeons and bullfights in his notebooks. Every day was a battle. Carmen, the family servant, was able to get him to school by force, but only after having accepted that he would bring a chicken with him in order to do its portrait. In class it was the same: he was restless all of the time, getting up, sitting down, getting up again,

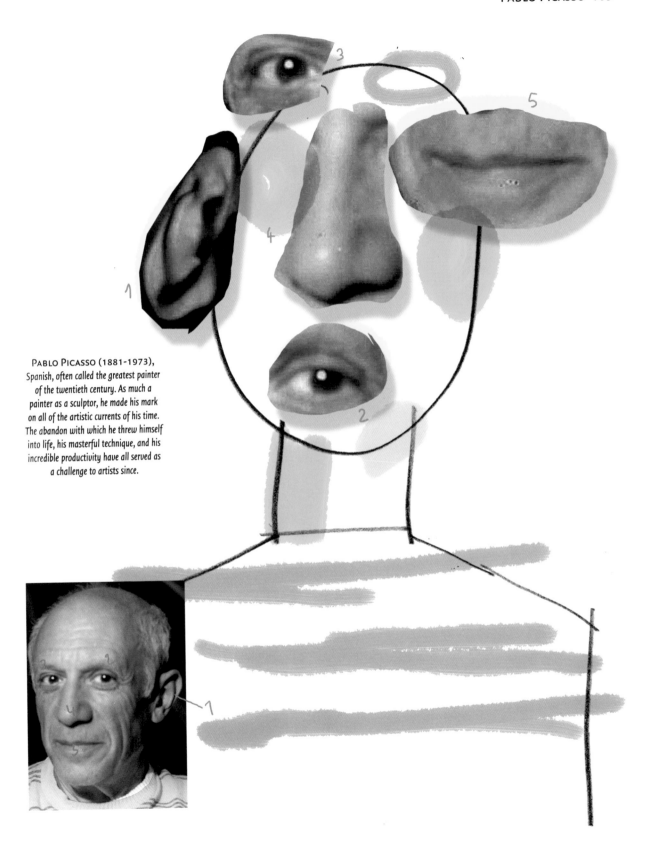

PABLO PICASSO (1881-1973), Spanish, often called the greatest painter of the twentieth century. As much a painter as a sculptor, he made his mark on all of the artistic currents of his time. The abandon with which he threw himself into life, his masterful technique, and his incredible productivity have all served as a challenge to artists since.

The word "Cubism" was invented by journalists who were scandalized by the paintings of Picasso and his friend Georges Braque, who searched and experimented in the same direction. The journalists attacked them by arguing that Picasso and Braque were content to merely associate cubes or other geometric forms on their canvases.

going to the window and calling out to the passers by. He even left his classroom to go to the principal's suite in order to get a closer look at the principal's wife, whom he found as beautiful as a fandango dancer. Already. As a result of his behavior, he was frequently punished. Turning this to his own advantage, he went so far as to get himself locked in an empty closet nicknamed, "the prison," so that he would be able to draw in peace. "*I would draw, draw, draw. I could have stayed there eternally without stopping.*"

Since the situation at school continued to deteriorate and Pablo's health had always been fragile, his father decided to take him out of school and engage a tutor. The result: no result. No progress. Pablo remained useless at schoolwork, but continued to draw constantly, abandoning his dear pigeons for human figures. He even began to elaborate portraits beginning from a single trait. He was only eight years old when he painted his first canvas—a picador—in oils. It should be noted, however, that he was not a precocious genius, just a "*genius of childhood,*" as he later would say.

As bad luck would have it, Pepe lost his job at the museum. The family thus had to move to the other side of Spain, to Corogne. Pablo was sent back to school, but with no more success. There was, however, a silver lining. In the same building as his school there was an art school, in which he enrolled. By the time he was thirteen, he had his first solo exhibition, thanks to a doctor friend of his parents. A year later, he received a "*lamentable*" mention from his high school, but a "*very good*" from art school.

Moreover, because he didn't like to write, he created a

drawing journal, *Azul y Blanco* (Blue and White), to send news to his family members in Malaga. In short, Pablo worked hard and acquired a solid artistic education. Indeed, his abilities were so great, that his father ceased to paint. *"At this time, he gave me his paints and brushes and never painted again."*

What happened next? Tragically, Pablo's little sister, Conchita, died of dyptheria. High drama and sorrow ensued, and the family left Corogne. Fortunately, Pepe received an appointment to La Lonja, the school of fine arts in Barcelona, where naturally enough he enrolled his youngster. Despite this family tie, Pablo remained rowdy, distracted and completely uninterested in the classes he thought unnecessary. Nevertheless, his daunting talent and the rapidity of his hand stunned everyone. He painted a lot, always in an academic style, and exhibited, but still he was frequently bored. He liked Barcelona, however, and took to partying with his friends at Els Quatre Gats (tapas, paella and red wine), so much so that his father sent him away to Madrid, to the San Fernando Royal Academy. There, strongly opposed to his professors' methods, Pablo visited the painting studio only because it was heated. *"They have no common sense! They are just as I suspected. It's always the same: for painting, Vélasquez, for sculpture, Michelangelo. I'm not saying that it would be bad to work in one way or another, but it shouldn't be that because a style has worked for one person that everyone should do the same as he."*

Pablo felt free and wanted to be free.
Just a few more years and the world would see the rightness of his path.
Right on, Picasso!

Les Demoiselles d'Avignon

The first "Cubist" work
The Brothel of Avignon is what the first Cubist work was going to be called before being renamed, *Les Demoiselles d'Avignon (The Prostitutes of Avignon)*. It was not the subject matter itself, but the manner in which the five prostitutes at the center of the canvas were represented that caused the scandal. Picasso finished this painting in 1907. His friend Manolo, who had come to visit, saw the canvas and exclaimed, *"Listen, Pablo, if you went to collect your parents from the train station and they arrived with faces similar to these you would not be happy."*

FRANÇOIS TRUFFAUT

Once the facts are known, it has to be admitted that François' childhood wasn't that of a healthy, happy kid. Born in Paris in 1932, he was the offspring of an unknown father and Janine de Montferrand, who was barely twenty. As Janine belonged to an upstanding Catholic family, his birth was concealed and he was sent away to a wet nurse. A year later, Janine married Roland Truffaut, who recognized François and gave him his surname. Nonetheless, François remained with his wet nurse until he was nearly three. Meanwhile, another baby was born, but he died after only two months. Suddenly, François was an unwanted only child—an embarrassment, a reminder of gloomy times, and unloved. He was off to a risky start.

Fortunately, his grandmother Geneviève decided to take him in. She raised him along with her last two children. François hardly ever saw his parents, which was just as well. His mother—independent, cultivated and elegant, spent her free time going to the cinema or with her lovers. His father, an architect, was a kind man with a sense of humor, but completely wrapped up in his mountaineering activities. François, who was small, sickly and "*alternated between vivaciousness and melancholy,*" spent most of his time chatting with his grandmother. At school, everything went well to begin with.

In the autumn of 1939 when France entered the war, the men in the Montferrand family were drafted, so Geneviève decided to stay with the children in Brittany when summer vacation ended. Much to her surprise, François, who was just seven, became difficult and disobedient. At her wit's end, she wrote to his mother of his "*unruly, inattentive, contentious mood,*" which would make her "*frantic*" if not "*nipped in the bud.*" When they returned

FRANÇOIS TRUFFAUT
(1932-1984), French filmmaker, made personal films that are all intimations of childhood, even if not explicitly so. With The 400 Blows, he created the character of Antoine Doinel, his alter ego, who appeared in five other films.

zéro plus zéro egale la tête à Truffaut

The 400 Blows.

Truffaut's first film, was released in 1959. It tells the story of Antoine Doinel, age fourteen. Faced with an unmaternal mother and a weak and passive father, Antoine takes refuge in lying and is seen as a delinquent by everyone. He is sent to reform school, but manages to escape. Truffaut's challenge was to make "*a kid who does a dishonest thing every five minutes*" lovable. The film triumphed and the character of Antoine was taken to heart. "*We bet that people would be entirely favorable to him and hostile to the parents.*" People identified with Antoine. The film's success also had to do with the spontaneity with which it was made. This approach to film, which came to be called "the new wave," involved quickly filming unknown actors with very little material far from the studios.

A still from the film The 400 Blows

to Paris a year later, François continued to be a good student, but his bad behavior continued as well. As one teacher wrote, "*He has no trouble understanding anything except discipline....*" Highly independent and given to sullen moods, he took to tramping around his neighborhood alone.

Sadly, his grandmother died when he was ten. He thus had to live with his parents, who looked on him as nothing more than a chore. Whenever a vacation came around they asked, "*What should we do with the kid?*" François suffered from this quasi-abandonment by becoming cyclothymic (alternating periods of elation and depression), irritable, and thin skinned. His beautiful mother fascinated him, but he hated her because she treated him (her "*little imbecile*") like hired help. So things went until age twelve, when he learned that Roland wasn't really his dad. With that, things took a disastrous turn.

He took to drifting around the streets of Paris, stealing from his parents' savings, and lying through his teeth, none of which went over very well, either at school or home. When he failed a test required for entry into 6th grade, he was offered the chance to retake it, but his parents neglected to bring him back to Paris for the test. As a result, he couldn't return to his old school, but had to go to the neighborhood school, where he really started to get into trouble. At fourteen, having "attended" three different schools, he passed from disobedience to rebellion to outright revolt. Nevertheless, he managed to obtain his certificate of studies. Often absent from school (he was nicknamed "the meteor"), he cut classes to sit in the city squares and read. For him, "*...school, instead of being educational, was an environment for fabricating lies, for creative falsifications; if classes had to be cut in order to read Balzac or Dumas, if playing hooky was* required in order to experience real life, then the thing to do was to defy authority and lie...." As an excuse, he went so far as to say that his mother had died. He lied constantly and ran away frequently. Suspicious of the self-righteous and the powerful, he no longer believed in the word of adults.

Luck, however, was on his side, this time in the person of Robert Lachenay, the last in the class, a devoted practitioner of hooky and the Leonardo da Vinci of the excuse. Inseparable, they tramped through the streets, slept in the same maid's room at the Lachenay's, pilfered from church offerings, discussed literature, and fell in love with the movies. François' passion was such that he saw Renoir's *Rules of the Game* twelve times. In the evenings they waited for Robert's parents to go out before leaving to slip into the darkened cinema. By age twelve, François was seeing 2-3 films a week. "*I saw my first two hundred films on the sly playing hooky and slipping into the movie house without paying.... I paid for these great pleasures with stomachaches, cramps, nervous headaches and guilty feelings, which only heightened the emotions evoked by the films.*" François and Robert even produced a magazine of film listings that they sold for pocket money. You can see all of this in Truffaut's film, *The 400 Blows*, a masterpiece that is sad and happy at the same time.

Thus François' own life began when he was barely fifteen, with Robert at his side. Small jobs, schemes, and theft were meshed with books, films, and the running of a film club. It was to support their club that they stole, went into debt and got into trouble with the police. At seventeen, François landed in a center for juvenile delinquents. Was there a silver lining? Not exactly, but at that dark moment, the shimmering hope of the silver screen lured him on. Clearly, he wasn't wrong to believe in it.

Truffaut and Jean-pierre Léaud, who appeared on screen as Antoine Doinel

A True Story?

Is your work inspired by your own life? This delicate question is often posed to artists. Truffaut's responses often contradicted each other. When *The 400 Blows* premiered at the Cannes Film Festival, he told the press that, yes, the movie had been inspired by his own life. He parents felt betrayed. His stepfather sent him a furious letter requesting an interview: "...you were so 'mistreated' by ignorant parents that they later allowed you to become a glorious and disinterested 'child martyr'." At other times, Truffaut gave a more nuanced reply: "I didn't write my biography in The 400 Blows." However, in 1973 he concluded, "The experiences of Antoine Doinel are mine and, I should add, without exaggeration."

BIBLIOGRAPHY

In addition to autobiographical writings (memoirs, letters), relevant novels and other writings, we also have included notable biographical works. Additionally, we have listed a number of websites for easily obtainable information and further links. Although some of these websites have been around for a while, please keep in mind that sites can change or virtually disappear overnight. The passages quoted in the biographical entries were drawn from the books listed below, largely from the autobiographical sources and interviews.

ARMSTRONG, LOUIS

Satchmo: My Life in New Orleans, by Louis Armstrong, Da Capo Press, 1986.

Louis Armstrong's New Orleans, by Thomas Brothers, W.W. Norton & Co., 2006.

Satchmo: The Genius of Louis Armstrong, by Gary Giddins, Da Capo Press, 2001.

Louis Armstrong: The Offstage Story of Satchmo, by Michael Cogswell, Collectors Press, 2003. (Official book of the Armstrong House & Archives. Includes 300 previously unpublished photos.)

Young Adult Choice: **Louis Armstrong: King of Jazz (African-American Biographies),** by Wendie C. Old, Enslow Publishers, 1998.

www.satchmo.net Official site of the Louis Armstrong House.

www.redhotjazz.com/louie.html Armstrong biography plus links to excellent pages on other jazz greats.

www.time.com/time/time100/ artists/profile/armstrong.html Time Magazine profile.

BALZAC, HONORÉ DE

Louis Lambert, by Balzac, Dodo Press, 2005.

Balzac, by Stefan Zweig, Viking, 1946.

Balzac: A Biography, by Graham Robb, W.W. Norton & Co, 1996.

Young Adult Choice: **Honoré de Balzac (Blooms Modern Critical Views),** by Harold Bloom, Chelsea House Publications, 2002.

Any of his novels.

BELL, ALEXANDER GRAHAM

Reluctant Genius: Alexander Graham Bell and the Passion for Invention, by Charlotte Gray, Arcade Publishing, 2006.

The Telephone Gambit: Chasing Alexander Graham Bell's Secret, by Seth Shulman, W.W. Norton, 2008.

Young Adult Choice: **Alexander Graham Bell: Making Connections** (Oxford Portraits in Science), by Naomi Pasachoff, OUP-USA, 1998.

www.alexandergrahambell.org A virtual library site with reference links and lots of solid information.

BUFFON

Buffon: A life in Natural History, by Jacques Roger, Cornell University Press, 1997.

From Natural History to the History of Nature: Readings from Buffon and His Critics, by John Lyon, Phillip R. Sloan, University of Notre Dame Press, 1981.

368 Animal Illustrations from Buffon's Natural History, by G.L. Buffon, Dover, 1993.

Buffon, by Pierre Gascar, Gallimard, 1983 (In French)

Buffon, by Jacques Roger, Fayard, 1989. (In French)

CÉZANNE, PAUL

Cézanne: A Biography, by John Rewald, Abrams, 1996.

Conversations with Cézanne, by Michael Doran, U of California Press, 2001.

Paul Cézanne, Letters, Edited by John Rewald, Da Capo, 2000.

Letters on Cézanne, by Rainer Maria Rilke, North Point Press, 2002.

Cézanne and Provence: The Painter in His Culture, by Nina Maria Athanassoglou-Kallmyer. U of Chicago Press, 2003.

Young Adult Choice: **Paul Cézanne: A Painter's Journey**, by Robert Burleigh & the National Gallery, Abrams, 2006.

CHAPLIN, CHARLIE
My Autobiography, by Charlie Chaplin, Penguin, 2003.

Charlie Chaplin: Interviews, by Kevin J. Hayes, Charlie Chaplin, U. Press of Mississippi, 2005.

The Essential Chaplin: Perspectives on the Life and Art of the Great Comedian, by Richard Schickel, Ivan R. Dee, 2006.

Chaplin: Genius of the Cinema, by Jeffrey Vance, Abrams, 2003.

Silent Traces: Discovering Early Hollywood through the Films of Charlie Chaplin, by John Bengtson, Kevin Brownlow, Santa Monica Press, 2006.

http://chaplin.bfi.org.uk
Excellent biography, filmography & more.
www.charliechaplin.com Official site.

CHARLEMAGNE
The Life of Charlemagne, by Einhard, U. of Michigan Press, 1960.

Becoming Charlemagne: Europe, Baghdad, and the Empires of A.D. 800, by Jeff Sypeck, Ecco, 2006.

Charlemagne: Father of a Continent, by Alessandro Barbero, U. of California Press, 2004.

Young Adult Choice: **Charlemagne (Ancient World Leaders)**, by Dale Evva Gelfand, Chelsea House Publications, 2003.

CHRISTIE, AGATHA
An Autobiography, by Agatha Christie, HarperCollins, 2001.

Come, Tell Me How You Live, by Agatha Christie Mallowan, Akadine Press, 2002.

The Complete Christie: An Agatha Christie Encyclopedia, Matthew Bunson, Pocket, 2000.

Young Adult Choice: **Agatha Christie: Writer of Mystery,** by Carol Dommermuth-Costa, Lerner Publications, 1997.

www.agathachristie.com Official Agatha Christie website.

Any of her books.

CHURCHILL, WINSTON
My Early Life, 1874-1904, by Winston Churchill, Touchstone, 1996.

The Last Lion: Winston Spencer Churchill, Visions of Glory, 1874-1932, by William Manchester, Little Brown, 1983.

The World Crisis, 1911-1918, by Winston Churchill, Free Press, 2005.

Young Adult Choice: **Winston Churchill: Soldier, Statesman, Artist**, by John B. Severance, Clarion Books, 1996.

www.time.com/time/time100/leaders/profile/churchill.html
Time Magazine profile.

www.bbc.co.uk/history/historic_figures/churchill_winston.html
BBC pages on Chuchill

DA VINCI, LEONARDO
Leonardo's Notebooks, by Leonardo da Vinci, H. Anna Suh, Black Dog & Leventhal, 2005.

The Lives of the Artists, by Giorgio Vasari, OUP-USA, 1998.

Leonardo da Vinci: Experience, Experiment and Design by Martin Kemp, Princeton University Press, 2006.

Leonardo da Vinci: The Marvelous Works of Nature and Man, by Martin Kemp, OUP-USA, 2007 **Leonardo**, by Martin Kemp, OUP-USA, 2005.

Young Adult Choice: **First Impressions: Leonardo da Vinci**, by Richard McLanathan, Abrams, 1990.

Young Adult Novel: **Leonardo's Shadow: Or, My Astonishing Life as Leonardo da Vinci's Servant,** by Christoper Gray, Atheneum, 2006.

http://www.mos.org/leonardo/ Boston Museum of Science's Leonardo site.

www.bbc.co.uk/science/leonardo The BBC's Leonardo homepage.

www.museoscienza.org/English/ Leonardo/ The Leonardo site of the Museum of Science and Technology in Milan.

DALI, SALVADOR
The Secret Life of Salvador Dali (Volume 1, autobiography), by Salvador Dali, Dover, 1993.

Diary of A Genius (Volume 2, autobiography), by Salvador Dali, J.G. Ballard, Solar Books, 2007.

Maniac Eyeball: The Unspeakable Confessions of Salvador Dali (Volume 3, autobiography), by Salvador Dali, Andre Parinaud, Creation Books, 2004.

Oui: The Paranoid-Critical Revolution, by Salvador Dali, Exact Change, 2004.

The Persistence of Memory: A Biography of Dali, by Meredith Etherington-Smith, Da Capo, 1995

www.salvadordalimuseum.org Official website of the Dali Museum.

DARWIN, CHARLES
The Autobiography of Charles Darwin, 1809-1882, by Charles Darwin, W. W. Norton, 1993.

The Voyage of the Beagle, by Charles Darwin, Modern Library, 2001.

Darwin: The Life of A Tormented Evolutionist, by Adrian Desmond and James Moore, Norton, 1994.

Charles Darwin: Voyaging, by E. Janet Browne, Princeton U Press, 1996.

Charles Darwin: The Power of Place, by E. Janet Browne, Princeton U Press, 2003.

Darwin's Origin of Species, A Biography, by E. Janet Browne, Atlantic Monthly Press, 2007.

http://darwin-online.org.uk Contains Darwin's complete publications, thousands of handwritten manuscripts and the largest bibliography available.

www.darwinfoundation.org Founded in 1959 under the auspices of UNESCO and the International Union for the Conservation of Nature and Natural Resources.

DAVID-NÉEL, ALEXANDRA
My Journey to Lhasa, by Alexandra David-Néel, Harper Perennial, 2005.

Magic and Mystery in Tibet, by Alexandra David-Néel, Book Tree, 2000.

The Secret Oral Teachings in Tibetan Buddhist Sects, by Alexandra David-Néel, City Lights Books, 1981.

Immortality and Reincarnation: Wisdom from the Forbidden Journey, by Alexandra David-Néel, Inner Traditions, 1997.

The Secret Lives of Alexandra David-Néel: A biography of the Explorer of Tibet and Its Forbidden Practices by Barbara M. Foster & Michael Foster, Overlook, 2002.

Tibet: Journey to the Forbidden City: Retracing the Steps of Alexandra David-Néel, by Tiziana Baldizzone, Gianni Baldizzone, et al., Stewart, Tabori & Chang, 1996.

Alexandra David-Néel: Portrait of An Adventurer, by Ruth Middleton, Shambala 1989.

www.alexandra-david-neel.org/anglais/acca.htm Official David-Néel website (English-language version).

DEBUSSY, CLAUDE
Debussy Remembered by Roger Nichols & Debussy, Amadeus Press, 2003.

Debussy Letters, by Roger Nichols & François Lesure, Harvard U. Press, 1987.

The Life of Debussy (Musical Lives), by Roger Nichols, Cambridge, 1998.

Young Adult Choice: **Claude Debussy (Composer's World),** by Wendy Thompson, Viking Juvenile, 1993.

DISNEY, WALT
The Animated Man: A life of Walt Disney, by Michael Barrier, University of California Press, 2007.

Hollywood Cartoons: American Animation in Its Golden Age, Michael Barrier, Oxford University Press, 1999.

Walt Disney: An American Original, by Bob Thomas, Hyperion, 1994.

Walt Disney: The Triumph of the American Imagination, by Neal Gabler, Knopf, 2006.

Once Upon A time: Walt Disney, The Sources of Inspiration for the Disney Studios, by Bruno Girveau, Prestel Publishing, 2007.

Walt Disney and the American Way of Life, Steven Watts, University of Missouri Press, 2001.

Young Adult Choice: **The Story of Walt Disney: Maker of Magical Worlds,** by Bernice Selden, Yearling, 1989.

DUMAS, ALEXANDRE
Alexandre Dumas, the King of Romance, by F .W. J Hemmings, Charles Scribner's, 1979.

The Titians: A Three-Generation Biography of the Dumas, by André Maurois, Trans. by Gerard Hopkins, Harper & Row, 1957.

Young Adult Choice: **Alexandre Dumas: Genius of Life,** by Claude Schopp, Franklin Wats, 1988.

The Three Musketeers, by Alexandre Dumas, Translator Richard Peaver, Penguin, 2007.

The Count of Monte Cristo, by Alexandre Dumas, Penguin, 2003

www.dumaspere.com/pages/english/sommaire.html English language home page of the Alexandre Dumas Society.

www.cadytech.com/dumas/ A rich compendium of information on Dumas

DUNANT, HENRY
Dunant's Dream: War, Switzerland, and the History of the Red Cross, by Caroline Moorehead, Carroll & Graf, 1999.

www.icrc.org/web/eng/siteeng0.nsf/htmlall/p0361?opendocument PDF download of Henry Dunant's book, **The Battle of Solferino.**

http://www.icrc.org/eng English-language website of the International Committee of the Red Cross. Search by: Henry Dunant, Geneva Conventions, Battle of Solferino.

EDISON, THOMAS
The Wizard of Menlo Park: How Thomas Alva Edison Invented the Modern World, by Randall E. Stross, Crown, 2007.

Edison: A Life of Invention, by Paul Israel, Wiley, 2000.

Thomas Edison and Modern America: A Brief history with Documents, by Lisa Gitelman, Theresa M. Collins, Bedford/St. Martins, 2002.

Young Adult Choice: **Thomas Alva Edison: The King of Inventors (Scientists & Inventors Series),** by David C. King, Discovery Enterprises, 1997.

http://edison.rutgers.edu The Edison Papers, over 5 million pages of documents.

EINSTEIN, ALBERT
Einstein: His Life and Universe, by Walter Isaacson, Simon & Schuster, 2007.

Relativity: The Special and General Theory, by A. Einstein, Penguin, 2007.

A Stubbornly Persistent Illusion: The Essential Scientific Works of Albert Einstein, Ed. & Commentary by Stephen Hawking, Running Press, 2007.

Super Cerveaux by Robert Clark PUF, 2001. (In French)

Young Adult Choice: **Genius: A Photobiography of Albert Einstein,** by Marfe Ferguson Delano, National Geographic, 2005.

Young Adult Choice: **Einstein: Visionary Scientist,** by John B. Severance, Clarion Books, 1999.

FLAUBERT, GUSTAVE
The Letters of Gustave Flaubert, 1830-1857, Selected, Edited and Translated by Francis Steegmuller, The Belknap Press of Harvard University, 1982.

Flaubert, by Henri Troyat, Viking, 1992.

Flaubert: a Biography, by Frederick Brown, Harvard University Press, 2007.

www.liv.ac.uk/soclas/los/madman.pdf Mémoires d'un fou/Memoirs of a Madman in French and English, written when he was young about his early life.

Bouvard and Pécuchet, by Gustave Flaubert, Translated by Mark Polizzotti, Dalkey Archive Press, 2005.

Madame Bovary, by Gustave Flaubert, Translated by Francis Steegmuller, Vintage, 1992.

GOUGES, OLYMPE DE
The Women of Paris and their French Revolution, by Dominique Godineau, U of California Press, 1998.

Rebel Daughters: Women and the French Revolution, Sara Melzer and Leslie Rabine, editors, OUP-USA, 1992

Young Adult Choice: **Women in History: Women of the French Revolution**, by Thomas Striessguth, Lucent, 2004.

Young Adult Choice: **International Encyclopedia of Women's Suffrage**, by June Hannam, Katherine Holden and Mitzi Auchterlonie, ABC-Clio, 2000.

www.library.csi.cuny.edu/dept/americanstudies/lavender/decwom2. html **Declaration of the Rights of Women**

LENNON, JOHN
All We Are Saying: The Last Major Interview with John Lennon & Yoko Ono, by David Sheff, St. Martin's Griffin, 2000.

John Lennon in His Own Words, by John Lennon, Barry Miles, Pearce Marchbank, Omnibus Press, 1990.

In His Own Write, by John Lennon, Yoko Ono, Simon & Schuster, 2000.

Lennon Remembers, by Jann S. Wenner, John Lennon, W.W. Norton & Co., 2001.

Lennon, The Definitive Biography by Ray Coleman, Harper Paperback, 1992.

John Lennon: The New York Years by Bob Gruen, Stewart, Tabori, & Chang, 2005.

Shout! The Beatles in Their Generation, by Philip Norman, Fireside, 2003.

Young Adult Choice: **Skywriting by Word of Mouth,** by John Lennon, Harper, 1987.

Young Adult Choice: **John Lennon: All I want is the Truth,** by Elizabeth Partridge, Viking Juvenile, 2005.

www.johnlennon.com The official Lennon website, courtesy of Yoko Ono.

www.lennon.net The official website of the Liverpool Lennons

www.taisei.co.jp/museum/index_e.html John Lennon Museum website.

LINCOLN, ABRAHAM
Abraham Lincoln: Speeches and Writings, Vol. I (1832-1858) and Vol. II (1859-1965), A. Lincoln & Don Fehrenbacher, Library of America, 1989.

Lincoln: The Presidential Archives; Intimate Photographs, Personal Letters, and Documents that Changed History, by Chuck Wills. DK, 2007.

Lincoln on Lincoln, Selected and Edited by Paul M. Zall, University Press of Kentucky, 1999.

With Malice Toward None: A life of Abraham Lincoln, by Stephen B. Oates, Harper Perennial, 1994.

Team of Rivals: The Political Genius of Abraham Lincoln, by Doris K. Goodwin, Simon & Schuster, 2006.

Lincoln in the Times: The Life of Abraham Lincoln as Originally Reported in The New York Times, by David Herbert Donald & Harold Holzer, St Martin's Press, 2005.

Young Adult Choice: **Lincoln's Melancholy: How Depression Challenged the President and Fueled His Greatness,** by Joshua Wolf Shenk, Houghton Mifflin, 2005

Young Adult Choice: **Abraham Lincoln and the Second American Revolution,** by James McPherson, OUP-USA, 1992.

LONDON, JACK
Jack: An Autobiography of Jack London, by Andrew Sinclair, Pocket, 1979.

John Barleycorn or, Alcoholic Memoirs, by Jack London, Signet Classics, 1990.

The Portable Jack London, by Jack London, Penguin, 1994.

Young Adult Choice: **Jack London: A biography,** by Daniel Dyer, Scholastic, 2002.

http://london.sonoma.edu The Jack London Online Collection

www.jacklondons.net The World of Jack London

PICASSO, PABLO
A Life of Picasso: The Prodigy, 1881-1906, by John Richardson, Knopf, reprint edition, 2007.

A Life of Picasso: The Cubist Rebel, 1907-1916, by John Richardson, Knopf, reprint edition, 2007.

A Life of Picasso: The Triumphant Years, 1917-1932, by John Richardson, Knopf, 2007.

The Ultimate Picasso, by Brigitte Leal, Christine Piot, Marie-Laure Bernadac, Harry N. Abrams, 2003.

Picasso, 200 Masterpieces from 1898 to 1972, by Pablo Picasso, Bernard Picasso, Bernie Rose, Bulfinch, 2002.

Picasso on Art: A selection of Views, by Pablo Picasso, Dore Ashton, Da Capo, 1988.

Young Adult Choice: **First Impressions: Pablo Picasso,** by John Beardsley, Abrams, 1991.

www.museupicasso.bcn.es/eng/index_eng.htm Site for the Picasso Museum, Barcelona. English-language version.

www.musee-picasso.fr Site for the Picasso Museum, Paris. In French, but great images.

TRUFFAUT, FRANÇOIS
Truffaut: A Biography, by Antoine de Baecque & Serge Toubiana, U of Califonia Press, 2000.

Truffaut by Truffaut, by François Truffaut, Abrams, 1987.

François Truffaut Interviews, Edited by Ronald Bergan, University of Mississippi/Jackson, 2008.

PICTURE CREDITS

ARMSTRONG, Pages 10-13
Drawing by Serge Bloch after a photo-graphic portrait of Armstrong, Getty/Time & Life Pictures/Eliot Elisofon.
Storyville, Getty/Hulton Archive

BALZAC, Pages 14-17
Drawing by Serge Bloch, portrait of Honoré de Balzac, anonymous pastel based on a daguerreotype of 1842. Balzac Museum, Paris. © AKG Images.
Illustration by Honoré Daumier for *Pere Goriot* , print by Baulant, National Library of France, Paris. © Gallimard archives.
A rooming house in Paris around 1845, *Five Floors of the Parisian World*, illustra-tion by Charles Berthall, 1852. © Kharbine-Tapabor/GR+Ma

BELL, Pages 18-21
Conversation: "Morality, Tranquility and Happiness, the Telephone Office," lithograph by Robida, appeared in *The Twentieth Century*, 1884. © Kharbine-Tapabor.
Drawing by Serge Bloch, photographic portrait of Bell around 1915. © Corbis.
The Beginning of the Telephone, engraving. © Gallimard archives.

BUFFON, Pages 22-25
Zebra, plate from Buffon's *Natural History, General and Particular*, 1774. © Gallimard archives.
Drawing by Serge Bloch, *Monsieur Buffon* illustration appeared in E. Mennechet's *Le Plutarque français*, 1835.

Library of Decorative Arts, Paris. © Bridgeman-Giraudon/Archives Charmet.
The African caravan in the Grand Hall of the National Museum of Natural History, Paris. © MNHN/Laurent Bessol.

CÉZANNE, Pages 26-29
Drawing by Serge Bloch, *Self-Portrait with Hat*, painting by Cézanne, 1879-1882. Kunstmuseum, Berne. © Bridgeman-Giraudon.
A Modern Olympia, painting by Cézanne, 1873-74. Musée d'Orsay, Paris. © RMN/Hervé Lewandowski.
Apples and Biscuits (detail), painting by Cézanne, 1877. Private Collection. © Bridgeman-Giraudon.

CHAPLIN, pages 30-33
Drawing by Serge Bloch.
Photo still pulled from Chaplin's film 1A.M., 1916. © Roy Export Co.Photo pulled from Chaplin's film *The Great Dictator*, 1940. © Roy Export Co.

CHARLEMAGNE Pages 34-37
Drawing by Serge Bloch, reliquary bust of Charlemagne offered in 1349 by Charles VI, Cathedral Treasury, Aix-la-Chapelle. © AKG Images/Erich Lessing
Charlemagne and his army crossing the Alps in 800. Liebig, chromo from the beginning of the 20th century.
© Leemage/Selva
Charlemagne's monogram, National Archives, Paris. © Bridgeman Giraudon/Archives Charmet

CHRISTIE, Pages 38-41
Drawing by Serge Bloch, photographic portrait of Agatha Christie in 1970. © Photoshot.
Excavations at the foot of the Giza Sphinx in Egypt at the beginning of the 20th century. © Gallimard archives.
Photo of Peter Ustinov in the role of Hercule Poirot in John Guillermin's film of *Death on the Nile*, 1978. © Collection Christophe L.

CHURCHILL, Pages 42-45
Drawing by Serge Bloch, photographic portrait of Churchill in his office in 1947. © Getty/Time Life Pictures/Nat Farbman.
A walk in Lambeth Way in London after a bombing in 1940. © Corbis.

DA VINCI, Pages 46-51
Drawing by Serge Bloch, *Portrait of a Bearded Man*, red chalk, by Leonardo da Vinci around 1513. Bibleoteca Reale, Turin. © Bridgeman-Giraudon.
Man the Measure of All Things, drawing by Leonardo around 1490. Galleria dell'Academia, Venice. © Bridgeman-Giraudon.
Mona Lisa, painting by Leonardo, 16th century. Louvre Museum, Paris. © RMN/Hervé Lewandowski-Thierry Le Mage

DALI, Pages 52-55
Drawing by Serge Bloch, photographic portrait of Dali © Roger-Viollet
Lobster Telephone © Bridgeman-Giraudon © Salvador Dali, Fondation

THE AUTHORS

A big name in French detective fiction, **Jean-Bernard Pouy** turns his attention here to some real life characters. For him, the happiest part of working on *The Big Book of Dummies, Rebels and Oher Geniuses* was realizing that there is no determinism: a problematic childhood, a failed education, an imposed or rejected profession can often lead to illumination.

After working for a time at a university press, **Anne Blanchard** needed a break. Interested in children's books and popular titles, she became an editor of illustrated books and… an author.

Serge Bloch, a recent transplant to New York, does wry and whimsical illustrations for newspapers and magazines as well as adult and children's books. He excels at overturning icons and more and more *"likes to combine illustration with photography because a photo really makes us believe that it's true. Often a single photographic element provides a sense of reality and drawing allows that to be played with."*

Acknowledgements

Idea: Anne Blanchard/Marque de Fabrique, with the invaluable cooperation
of Thomas Dartigue, managing editor, Documentary Department, Gallimard Jeunesse

Art Direction: Élisabeth Cohat and Raymond Stoffel

Cover Design: Serge Bloch and Raymond Stoffel

Editor for Documentary Entries: Anne Blanchard

Biographical and Documentary Research: Karine Siméon and
Charles Montmasson/Marque de Fabrique

Picture Research: Valérie Delchambre/Électron libre

Editors: Jeanne Hély and Clotilde Oussiali

Copyediting: Jocelyne Marziou and Isabelle Haffen

For their work on the Enchanted Lion Books edition,
special thanks go to Millicent Fairhurst and Abigail Bedrick.

Photogravure: IGS
Printed by Midas Printing International Limited